Create the Perfect Brand

Teach Yourself®

Create the Perfect Brand

Julia Hitchens and
Paul Hitchens

For UK order enquiries: please contact Bookpoint Ltd,
130 Milton Park, Abingdon, Oxon OX14 4SB.
Telephone: +44 (0) 1235 827720. Fax: +44 (0) 1235 400454.
Lines are open 09.00–17.00, Monday to Saturday, with a 24-hour
message answering service. Details about our titles and how to
order are available at www.teachyourself.com

Long renowned as the authoritative source for self-guided learning –
with more than 50 million copies sold worldwide – the **Teach Yourself**
series includes over 500 titles in the fields of languages, crafts, hobbies,
business, computing and education.

British Library Cataloguing in Publication Data: a catalogue record
for this title is available from the British Library.

This edition published 2010.

The **Teach Yourself** name is a registered trade mark of Hodder Headline.

Typeset by MPS Limited, A Macmillan Company.

Printed in Great Britain for Hodder Education, an Hachette UK
Company, 338 Euston Road, London NW1 3BH, by CPI Cox &
Wyman, Reading, Berkshire RG1 8EX.

The publisher has used its best endeavours to ensure that the URLs for
external websites referred to in this book are correct and active at the
time of going to press. However, the publisher and the author have
no responsibility for the websites and can make no guarantee that a
site will remain live or that the content will remain relevant, decent or
appropriate.

Hachette UK's policy is to use papers that are natural, renewable
and recyclable products and made from wood grown in sustainable
forests. The logging and manufacturing processes are expected to
conform to the environmental regulations of the country of origin.

| Impression number | 10 9 8 7 6 5 4 3 2 1 |
| Year | 2014 2013 2012 2011 2010 |

Front cover: © Digifoto Green/Alamy

Back cover: © Jakub Semeniuk/iStockphoto.com, © Royalty-
Free/Corbis, © agencyby/iStockphoto.com, © Andy Cook/
iStockphoto.com, © Christopher Ewing/iStockphoto.com,
© zebicho – Fotolia.com, © Geoffrey Holman/iStockphoto.com,
© Photodisc/Getty Images, © James C. Pruitt/iStockphoto.com,
© Mohamed Saber – Fotolia.com

Dedication

For Guy and Miles

So throw off the bowlines.
Sail away from the safe harbor.
Catch the trade winds in your sails.
Explore. Dream. Discover.

Mark Twain

Contents

Meet the authors

This is a book about branding – but it's also about the realization of dreams. Through our experience of creating brands and by working with many entrepreneurs, we know that every great brand begins with a good idea. Keeping a positive mental attitude is essential for anyone considering the prospect of creating a perfect brand. The main motivation is never purely financial but is driven by passion. It takes courage to create a brand and there can be challenges on the route to success.

We started our own brand consultancy – Verve – in 1996. We chose the word 'verve' for its meaning – energy, enthusiasm and dynamism – all attributes needed for brand building. We advise and work with entrepreneurs and directors in a variety of organizations to deliver corporate brand strategies. Verve has had the privilege of working for some of the UK's leading companies, including Granada Media and Virgin Atlantic. We have created brands and provided creative services to many industry sectors including: broadcasting, education, local government, manufacturing, oil and training.

Between us we have over 40 years of professional experience. Julia is a Charted Marketer with The Chartered Institute of Marketing. Paul has contributed branding commentary to the national and trade press.

Paul studied Graphic Design at the London College of Printing and began his creative career in advertising, where he won awards for his work. Paul later worked for Wolff Olins on the General Motors (GM) brands of Vauxhall, Saab, Opel and North American Vehicles. Since forming Verve with Julia they have hosted seminars on the importance of building a strong brand.

Julia studied Business at the University of Greenwich and began her career in marketing with campaigns for Samsung and Telewest. She later worked on global brands including; MGF Rover and ICL.

Verve worked together with the British Science Association and the University of Surrey for the launch of the British Science Festival in 2009. We are an approved BBC 'Future Media Supplier' and in 2007 we took part as a design associate on the 'Designing Demand' Programme organized by the Design Council, SEEDA and Business Link.

We hope this book will be both educational and inspiring and will motivate you to create your perfect brand!

Julia Hitchens and Paul Hitchens

Only got a minute?

We drive them, wear them, eat them and live with them. They exert a powerful influence on our behaviour, but what are they? BRANDS!

A brand is a small word considering the big part they play in our lives. Brands are about our feelings; trust, pride, joy, excitement, security, love and even lust and greed. We love our brands and even join clubs to prove it – from owners clubs to fan clubs. Some brands are symbols of our love or hate – 'Marmite' defines both ends of the spectrum. We use brands to describe ourselves and identify like-minded people. They are symbols of self-expression that we use to gain acceptance to a club or social clique. Throughout the history of mankind, we have used branding to mark out our territory and proclaim tribal membership.

In a fast moving society, we use brands as a short cut to making decisions. Their reputation guides our choice in the process of selection. Today, every car brand offers the same basic benefits – trouble-free transport with a warranty and a proven level of safety. But we are prepared to pay much more for kudos, style and status. Trust in the brand name means you don't need to struggle with the details.

Brands offer a barrier to competition. They position themselves first in the mind so that there is no alternative. In every walk of life there is a brand leader that offers something more than just performance.

This book explains what they are, why you need one, what they are worth and how to build one. We have illustrated the book with real-life examples to help inspire you to create your perfect brand!

5 Only got five minutes?

If you ask a friend to tell you about their favourite things, chances are they will speak passionately about a brand. It could be a football club, make of car, music or holiday destination, but one thing's for certain, great brands are held close to the heart. In an age of mass consumerism filled with copycat products, it's the ones that stand apart and think differently that connect on a deeper level with customers. The scope of this book is wide and designed to give a holistic view of how to create a brand.

The book is divided into four sections:

1 Brand importance
2 Brand creation
3 Brand implementation
4 Brand support

Malcolm Gladwell, author of the bestseller *Outliers* (Allen Lane, 2008) writes that 'the best way to achieve success is to spend 10,000 hours honing your skills'. This is a factor many entrepreneurs will attest to. Behind every great brand story it is usual to find a tale of dedication; few, if any, achieve overnight success. We have all heard stories of famous musicians who began their careers by travelling the country in transit vans and performing at small venues before getting their big break. In business, it starts with prototyping and honing an idea before it achieves the winning formula that connects with the customer. Sir James Dyson spent years developing his dual-cyclone vacuum cleaner before achieving success and changing the marketplace by creating a new type of cleaner. This takes dedication and an overarching vision.

Whether you're a musician or an inventor, a clear vision is the distinguishing mark of success. It answers the question, 'What's the point and why am I doing this?' When everyone supports the vision – its purpose and values – it builds a cohesive culture that carries the brand forward. In such businesses, people are motivated by the vision and committed to it. They understand it and are able to share it with their colleagues, clients or customers. They know their contribution to the brand's success and can see its effect. It creates a sense of esteem and *esprit de corps* among the employees, and they identify themselves with the brand and are able to work together towards a shared goal.

Great brands are built on good manners and hospitality. Poor service will destroy a reputation. After all, who wants a wonderful restaurant meal if it means being served by a surly waiter and a table next to the toilets! *The Sunday Times* publishes an annual list of the best businesses to work for. Valued people feel happier and take pride in their work, which is critical because people bring a brand to life.

Every organization is required to identify itself, if only by name. That name becomes a symbol for the brand experience. If I say Coca-Cola you will have an immediate picture in your mind of the product. This identity plays a very important role in setting up the market stall. The name, colour, typography, imagery and symbols all prepare the market audience for the experience. To succeed the image must not deliver style over substance as this is a deception and will only have a short-term benefit. The logo is not the 'brand' but merely the means by which we identify the brand. If a picture is worth a thousand words, then the aesthetics of a corporate identity is invaluable in the recognition of a brand. From the Mercedes-Benz 'three-pointed star' to the Nike 'swoosh', symbols play an important role in helping us navigate our way to our favourite brands.

If branding is concerned with differentiation and identification, then sight must be the sense we rely on most. We are able to perceive infinite subtleties of colour yet the majority of businesses choose blue for their identity. Be it cyan, indigo, royal or sky, businesses choose blue more than any other colour for their brand identity. Visit any British trade fair and you will be bathed in blue.

So why, when you want your business to stand out, would you camouflage your brand? Colour is an asset that can become closely linked to the brand.

With Google the most popular search tool for online commerce, a carefully chosen word can mean the difference between being picked up by the search engine or obscurity. Whether it's a made-up name, an acronym or a family name, a successful brand name should be memorable, pronounceable and legible.

Small to medium-sized enterprises (SMEs) have yet to capitalize on the full potential of branding. At the start of 2008, the total number of SMEs in the UK was 4.8 million, which account for 99.9 per cent of all UK enterprises (Department for Business Innovation and Skills, Statistical Press Release, October 2009). The UK is very strong on creativity and it is a resource that is crying out for the SME sector to take advantage of. According to UCAS, Design Studies was the second most popular degree course in 2009 with 16,912 accepted applications (UCAS Media Release, January 2009). According to the Design Council report 'Design Industry Insights 2010' there are 82,500 design consultancies in the UK. The Design Council has also revealed that only 19 per cent of UK businesses work with outside agencies. The Creative Industries are the second largest industry in London after the business services sector.

So who are the people that will build tomorrow's new brands? They are the brand champions or entrepreneurs with the passion to inspire – it's no accident that charismatic leaders are behind some of the world's biggest brands, from Sir Richard Branson to Steve Jobs. It takes all types of people, but long-term success depends on commitment and verve.

We hope you will be inspired to create your perfect brand!

Acknowledgements

With special thanks and appreciation for all your love and support: Sheila and Howard Dowding, Catherine and John Hitchens.

We would also like to thank:

Paul Reynolds, David Kidwell, Victoria Lubbock, Peter Moody, Justin Potter, Giles Brake, Penny Stothard, Gavin Smith, Chris Richardson, Lisa Richardson, John Martin, Rachel Crane, Mark Trezona, Beata Maaga, June McLeod, Alison Frecknall, Jill Birch, Katie Roden and Dieter Rams.

Part one
Brand importance

1

What is a brand?

In this chapter you will learn about:
- *the definition of a brand*
- *the classification of brands*
- *brand history*
- *how brand is the heart and soul of a business*
- *the importance of past, present and future for a brand*
- *brand ownership*

Definition of a brand

Premier league football clubs are described as great brands and are owned by international entrepreneurs. Successful sportsmen, such as Michael Jordan and David Beckham, can become brands. The reality television programme *The Apprentice* has challenged candidates to create a brand in a week, and the experts on the popular BBC television series *Dragons' Den* frequently discuss the merits of a proposed business venture by its chances of becoming a 'strong brand'. So what exactly is a brand?

A brand is a powerful force that can influence people's behaviour. A brand is a feeling. It can connect with people emotionally and psychologically, guide consumer understanding of value and lead to loyalty. It is a valuable asset based on reputation. The term 'brand' traditionally covers products, services and organizations, but can include people, places and nations.

In the 1990s the UK got a rebrand. Tony Blair's New Labour government encouraged the 'Cool Britannia' branding that helped sell the UK's vibrant culture to a global audience. Artists, musicians and creative celebrities were invited to Downing Street and celebrated as champions of contemporary Britain. The union flag was rescued from its negative associations with right-wing politics and became the logo for 'Cool Britannia', appearing on everything from guitars to Ginger Spice!

The brand lives in the minds of those who believe in it. Its integrity is constantly put to the test through the experiences of consumers and the actions of employees. The popularity of online social networks places brands under ever-stronger scrutiny. Reputations can easily be broken and a brand cannot rest on its laurels. To achieve sustainability it must constantly innovate to remain relevant to the consumer.

A brand must come from the heart, be honest and true. It will not work if you contrive an image based on deception. Brands are not manufactured, but spring from the instincts of entrepreneurial spirit. Success is achieved by following a unique path with conviction. Having a clear vision is the only quality that unites successful brands, but each vision is unique.

The underlying idea behind a brand becomes the ethos that drives and shapes an organization. The brand becomes the compass to success, guiding decisions and strategy in a realization of its values.

Insight

In the majority of small- to medium-sized enterprises (SMEs), the brand is an extension of the founding entrepreneur's personality. The owner's passion comes through their business brand. A very successful illustration of this model is Virgin. The Virgin brand is an extension of Richard Branson's charismatic personality and the two are synonymous with each other.

Brands depend on their hard-earned reputation. We expect our Duracell batteries to go on and on, we expect Volvo to make safe cars and we expect that Gillette is the best a man can get. If our expectation is not satisfied then the brand promise has been compromised.

A brand eases the path to innovation, as consumers are more open to experiment with new ideas from a trusted source. They create a halo of confidence.

A logo is not a brand. Logos, trade marks and corporate identities are the visual signals that represent the values of a brand. A logo has a valuable role to play in building brand recognition; it is a facet of the brand but not the brand itself. The logo represents the brand and conveys its attributes; it authenticates and identifies but it is not a replacement for the experience.

Brands can be legally protected, bought, sold, franchised or licensed. It's difficult to place an exact value on a brand, but when you have one it can mean the difference between obscurity and international recognition, profit or loss.

Brands are used as signals of personal expression. They are symbols of status and shorthand for our loves and passions. We use them to identify ourselves and they provide a coded language for social awareness. We pigeon-hole people by the brands they choose. The car you drive, the clothes you wear, the newspaper you read, the postcode you live in – they are all brands and they brand you!

Brands it seems can be many things. So, is there an exact definition for what a brand is? If you speak to a group of consultants each one will give their own interpretation. Wally Olins, co-founder of brand consultancy Wolff Olins, describes a brand as a personality. Walter Landor, founder of brand consultants Landor Associates, defined a brand as a promise. And Al Ries, author of *The 22 Immutable Laws of Branding*, defines a brand as the concept of singularity. Hear are a few more definitions of brands and branding.

A brand is simply an organization, or a product, or a service with a personality.

Wally Olins, author of *The Brand Handbook*

Branding is ultimately about nothing more (and nothing less) than heart. It's about passion ... what you care about. It's about what's inside – what's inside you, what's inside your company.

Tom Peters, author of *Re-imagine*

Simply put, a brand is a promise. By identifying and authenticating a product or service it delivers a pledge of satisfaction and quality.

Walter Landor

A successful branding program is based on the concept of singularity. It creates in the mind of the prospect the perception that there is no product on the market quite like your product.

Al Ries and Laura Ries, authors of *The 22 Immutable Laws of Branding*

A brand is the totality of perceptions – everything you see, hear, read, know, feel, think, etc. – about a product, service or business.'

Philip Kotler and Waldemar Pfoertsch, authors of *B2B Brand Management*

Classification of brands

Brand architecture is a grandiose name for simplifying your business strategy into an easily understandable framework. There are three broad categories – single, endorsed and branded.

SINGLE BRAND MODEL

The most popular type of brand model is the single brand. The business will use a single name and identity throughout the organization. All products and services in a single brand carry the same single message.

Most small to medium-sized enterprises (SMEs) start as a single brand and stay that way. This strategy is easier to manage because every facet of the business supports a single idea. It is economical to implement and build on brand recognition through repeated exposure. The risk of this model is that a crisis leading to loss of reputation can affect the whole business.

Examples of single brands
Heinz: *Heinz Baked Beans, Heinz Spaghetti, Heinz Tomato Ketchup …*
Virgin: *Virgin Atlantic, Virgin Trains, Virgin Media.*

Insight
The 'Heinz 57 varieties' slogan was inspired by a train ride. Henry J. Heinz noticed an advert for a shoe store selling 21 styles. He had over 60 products but chose the number '57' because it combined his lucky number '5' with his wife's number '7'. The number '57' has continued to have special significance for the brand and even its postal address in Pittsburgh is PO Box 57.

ENDORSED BRAND MODEL

Endorsed brands usually form part of a portfolio of individual brands, each endorsed by its parent company. This structure is suited to acquisition and allows the investor to retain the loyalty and recognition of the acquired brand's customers, whilst placing it under the security of the parent name. The parent brand gives credibility and maintains its profile for the benefit of the shareholder.

Examples of the endorsed brand model
Nestlé: *Nestlé Shreddies, Nestlé Cheerios, Nestlé Milkybar etc.*
Kellogg's: *Kellogg's Frosties, Kellogg's Corn Flakes, Kellogg's Rice Krispies etc.*

BRANDED MODEL

The branded model is a portfolio of brands owned by a parent
company with a low brand profile. Quite often the customer will
be unaware that the product brand is part of a larger group, for
example Guinness is owned by Diageo. The branded model allows
the parent company to compete at different value points in the same
sector without harming consumer perception, e.g. Volkswagen
Group owns Skoda, Seat, Audi and Bentley. Each brand can be sold
without damaging consumer loyalty if the new custodian stays true
to the brand. The downside when this model succeeds is that the
parent company could be viewed as creating a market monopoly.

Examples of the branded model
Swatch: *Tissot, Longines, Omega, Breguet*
GlaxoSmithKline: *Macleans, Lucozade, Horlicks, Ribena.*

Note: There are exceptions to the rule and some global companies
will use a combination of these models, for example Kraft acquired
the Cadbury brand in 2010. The Kraft Foods brand portfolio is a
story of acquisition. It includes names that blur the boundaries of
brand architecture: Kraft Philadelphia, Terry's Chocolate Orange
and Toblerone.

Brand history

Brands have been guiding consumer choice for centuries. One of
television's most popular and enduring programmes, *The Antiques*

Roadshow, is a window on the evolution of the brand. It first aired on the BBC in 1979 and in the last 30 years has influenced many derivatives, including *Bargain Hunt* and *Cash in the Attic*. The show's success thrives on our curiosity and has made amateur experts of us all at identifying heritage brands. Viewers are invited to present their family heirlooms for identification. The experts on these shows are full of anecdotes about the craftspeople behind the antiques. They inform us about the lives of the goldsmith, carpenter or potter and provide insights into how the object was produced. By watching, we learn about the manufacturing and crafts industry of the past. Recognizing the maker's trade marks helps the identification of these products. The viewers are introduced to a coded world of symbols forming some of the earliest commercial trading marks which today we describe as logos. Many of the antiques on these shows originated from the studios and shop floors of brands that still thrive today. Antique brand names that still trade today include: Spode (est. 1770), Meisson (est. 1710), Wedgwood (est. 1759) and Lalique (est. 1885).

Trade marks have been used since antiquity. In the Roman era, bricks and tiles were embossed with trade marks made using oak or bronze stamps that declared the clay's origin or name of the manufacturer, contractor or emperor.

Branding is part of the human condition. Since the dawn of civilization we have been painting our bodies and tattooing our skin to communicate that we are different and belong to a distinct society or group. We have left giant marks on the landscape and placed symbols on our dwellings to signify our ideology.

The Uffington White Horse is an icon of the English landscape and an immediately recognizable symbol. The stylized horse is carved into the chalk of a dry valley. It is located close to the ancient Ridgeway Path and can be seen for miles leaping across the Oxfordshire landscape. A complete view of the horse is only possible from the air, which has led to theories that it was a sign to the gods. Historians have linked the White Horse with similar designs found on Iron Age coinage and suggested that the horse was the symbol of the same people that built nearby Uffington Castle. The horse became a symbol that identified these people – it was their corporate identity. Recent testing methods have dated the Uffington Horse to the late Bronze Age 3,000 years ago.

The Palaeolithic cave paintings in Lascaux, France, are over 32,000 years old. These symbolic illustrations of horses, bison and mammoths look so contemporary Pablo Picasso could have painted them. When the artist visited the newly discovered caves, in 1940, he said of modern art, 'We have discovered nothing.' Stone Age people lived by hunting and gathering and the painted symbols communicate their status as hunters and their way of life. Today people choose brands to communicate their status and aspirations. As the French Novelist Jean-Baptiste Alphonse Karr wrote, *'plus ça change, plus c'est la même chose'*: the more things change, the more they stay the same!

The origins of the word 'brand' can be traced back to the eighth century and the North-Germanic language of Old Norse. In its original form *brandr* translates as 'firebrand' or 'to burn'. The word was first used in a commercial sense when cattle owners began using heated irons to burn identifying marks in the hides of their livestock. This method of identification developed into a sophisticated variety of symbols in North America.

RECENT BRAND HISTORY

Today the logos of brands like Coca-Cola, McDonalds and Nike are instantly recognizable. They have been burnt into our consciousness and have left a permanent mark on our memory; their logos are understood around the globe. The last century has witnessed an explosion of brands vying for our attention. With the birth of new technology there is a scramble to be the leading brand in the new category. The birth of the motor car over a hundred years ago introduced some of the most emotive brands. Many of those pioneers are still relevant today.

Michelin

'Bibendum' the Michelin tyre man has been selling tyres for
the French brand since 1894. The brothers Edouard and André
Michelin were inspired by a stack of tyres they saw at the
Universal and Colonial Exposition in Lyon. Edouard thought
they resembled a large man without arms. André later met the
French cartoonist Marius Rossilon (also known as O'Galop) who
showed him a rejected concept for a brewery in Munich. André
suggested replacing the central character of a large aristocratic
man with a figure made of tyres. The cartoonist obliged and now
Bibendum is one of the world's most recognized trade marks.
Over the years Bibendum has been redrawn and slimmed down to
reflect prevailing taste. He continues to have popular appeal and
featured in one of the bestselling *Astérix* cartoon books *Astérix in
Switzerland*. In 2010 he has been brought right up to date fighting a
Transformer-style petrol pump in a computer generated television
advert extolling Michelin's fuel saving attributes.

Mercedes-Benz

Emil Jellinek was an Austrian businessman with an enthusiasm
for motoring who lived in Nice. In 1899 he entered and won the
'Tour de Nice' with a Daimler Car competing under his daughter's
name 'Mercedes'. Jellinek instigated with Wilhelm Maybach the
design of a new high-performance model for Daimler. He ordered
36 of the new cars and became the exclusive sales agent in certain
countries. Daimler agreed to Jellinek's suggestion that these
new cars be called Mercedes, and the Mercedes trade mark was
registered in 1902.

The Mercedes-Benz three-pointed star originates from a family
postcard sent by Gottlieb Daimler to his wife. Following Daimler's
death at 66, his two sons remembered the card, which featured
a star above the house that he had lived in. Daimler said that,
'this star would rise and shine out over his work'. In 1909 the

(Contd)

application to trade mark a three-pointed star and a four-pointed star were granted. Only the three-pointed star was used and it still shines over the marque today.

VINTAGE COMMERCIAL BRANDS

It may be surprising to learn that some of the brands we take for granted on a daily basis have such a long history:

Stella Artois	Belgium	1366	Brewer
Lloyd's of London	UK	1688	Insurance
Moët & Chandon	France	1743	Champagne
Guinness	Ireland	1759	Brewery
Birkenstock	Germany	1774	Shoes
Colgate	US	1806	Soap
Cadbury	UK	1824	Chocolate
Shell	Netherlands	1833	Petroleum
Procter & Gamble	US	1837	Consumer
Louis Vuitton	France	1854	Luggage
Burberry	UK	1856	Fashion
HSBC	Hong Kong	1865	Bank
Levi Strauss	US	1873	Clothing

Heart and soul – the core of a business

A brand is at the very core of a business and represents the heart and soul. It stands for the truth and must be authentic, inspiring, passionate and memorable.

From the very first experience, a brand's integrity is under test. Every detail, from the attitude of the telephone receptionist, to a book of helpful instructions will have an effect on the consumers' perception of the brand.

Brands are like a courtship, but the relationship will not last long if there are unwelcome surprises.

In March 2010 it was announced that the Chinese Auto Maker, Geely was buying the Volvo car brand. When asked to summarize what he liked about the brand, Founder and Chairman Li Shufu exclaimed, 'I love you'.

(Financial Times)

Past, present and future

A brand lives in three dimensions: the past, present and future. The past is its reputation, the present is the experience and the future is the expectation.

PAST – REPUTATION

Let's start with you. Your family and friends know what you look like, how you think and how you behave. If you do something unexpected or treat your friends poorly you understand that you may compromise your relationship. We all build a reputation with the people we are regularly in contact with. You can build that reputation or destroy it by your behaviour. It's a popular scenario in any television soap opera following a scandal: 'you have brought our family name into disrepute!' It's the same with a business, a product or a service. A brand is built on reputation.

In the age of the internet, it's easy to research if a brand has a good reputation. Most online trading sites encourage customers to write reviews of their purchases. A good review is an endorsement that attracts new customers and builds loyalty.

Ratners

In 1991, the CEO of Ratners jewellers, Gerald Ratner, gave a speech to the Institute of Directors at the Royal Albert Hall. He made the fatal mistake of joking about the quality of his products: he described a £4.95 Ratners decanter as 'total crap' and said the firm's 99p earrings were 'cheaper than a prawn sandwich from

(Contd)

Marks & Spencer, but probably wouldn't last as long!' The effect of his words devalued his business by £500 million! By branding his products 'crap' he wiped the value off the Ratners' share price. 'Doing a Ratner' has now become the term for business people who put their foot in it.

A brand for a company is like a reputation for a person. You earn reputation by trying to do hard things well. People notice that over time. I don't think there are any shortcuts.

Jef Bezos, Chief Executive of Amazon

Tiger Woods

Another spectacular fall from grace came with the serial adultery scandal of Tiger Woods. The world's number one golfer is a brand in his own right and even has his own logo and products. He is the subject of lucrative sponsorship deals with some of the world's largest brands including: Nike, Accenture, Gillette and Tag Heuer. Gillette became the first major sponsor to announce that Woods would 'play no further part in their marketing until he has sorted out his private life'. Woods' actions were not in keeping with his public persona and have compromised his position as an ambassador for the brands that sponsor him. The 'Tiger Woods' brand has been carefully managed and the awkward home truths were kept out of the media.

The inevitability of any brand (corporate, product or service) is that the truth will out.

It takes many good deeds to build a good reputation, and only one bad one to lose it.

Benjamin Franklin, one of America's founding fathers

PRESENT – EXPERIENCE

The trading estates of Britain are the heartland of the UK's small to medium-sized enterprises (SMEs). Our experience is that they are often shabby and uninspiring. A typical business unit will have a badly signposted entrance that opens to a reception area with a worn and stained carpet. The connecting corridors are marked and tarnished. They can be dull places, but millions of people work in them. These businesses usually have a great product and a dedicated team but the environment lets them down.

The majority of SMEs in the UK do not pay attention to their brand. They may have a great business, but this is not reflected in how they present themselves to the outside world. We have frequently met business people whose eyes glaze over when you mention branding. They are proud that they have had success through their networks and personal contacts, and they maintain that customers buy from them personally and that the business brand is not an issue or priority. Their own personal branding is typically good, but they do not follow this through to their company. They usually drive a prestigious car and take care of their appearance but they pay little attention to their business brand. The brand should be reflected in every aspect of the business.

If a consumer has no knowledge of a product and if there is no previous experience to judge it by, then all that is left is visual appearance and presentation. First impressions are very powerful. Visual image has an important part to play in positioning a brand and preparing us for the experience. Of course if the experience is lacking then the brand will flounder. But what if you have a great product and the presentation is poor?

If we are to learn to improve the quality of the decisions we make, we need to accept the mysterious nature of our snap judgments.

Malcolm Gladwell, *Blink: The Power of Thinking Without Thinking*

How good are we at judging character? The rise of the talent show as a popular entertainment format has been a phenomenon throughout the first decade of the millennium. Shows like *Pop Idol*, *The X Factor* and *Britain's Got Talent* have been compelling viewing for many people and have catapulted unknowns into familiar household names.

In April 2009 the ITV talent show *Britain's Got Talent* clearly illustrated how first impressions can be so spectacularly wrong. When a dowdy middle-aged spinster called Susan Boyle took to the stage, the audience clearly indicated that they had low expectations; many people in the audience were cruelly mocking her. Susan Boyle did not match the stereotype of a successful female singer. She wasn't young and glamorous. As Susan Boyle began to sing 'I dreamed a dream' from the musical *Les Miserables* the smirking expressions seen in the members of the audience changed to open-mouthed shock. The panellists Piers Morgan, Amanda Holden and Simon Cowell were clearly in awe. Susan Boyle surprised everybody with a remarkable singing voice. The moment attracted international attention and was one of the most viewed clips on YouTube. On Sunday 29 November 2009, Susan Boyle had a number one album, which became the fastest-selling debut album of all time. 'I Dreamed A Dream' has sold more than 410,000 copies – a record for a first-week's sale of a debut album since records began. The media described the moment as a modern parable, teaching us not to judge by appearances.

So how good are we at judging character? Are we not all guilty of judging a book by its cover? Is your business a Susan Boyle business? There are many businesses that have a fantastic product or service but the visual presentation lets them down. A business may not get the opportunity to prove itself like Susan Boyle did and its image becomes a stumbling block to brand success.

The audience was obliged to listen to Susan Boyle. However, if Susan had been a business website, would the potential customer have given her a chance? Would they have clicked further into the site or would they have taken one look at the homepage and moved on?

Potential customers need to 'get' the brand in an instant. You want to make sure that everything you believe in comes across immediately. It is not easy to do this, as branding is so much more than a logo – service, environment, colour, imagery etc. all play a part. Your brand should be mirrored in every part of your company, from the product or service to the environment, people and culture.

FUTURE – EXPECTATION

Branding builds trust and confidence. A familiar brand carries with it an expectation of performance. Based on its reputation and frequent experience a consumer builds an expectation of how the brand will perform in the future. For example, when you visit your favourite restaurant you expect good service and an enjoyable evening based on past experience. If the service is poor or the food disappointing it will make you think twice about returning. Every business will encounter a crisis at some point, but it's how the crisis is handled that builds or sinks the brand.

UK Parliament
In May 2009, it was revealed that MPs of all parties had been regularly making inappropriate expense claims. This widespread misuse of taxpayers' money left the public feeling that their trust had been betrayed. Politics was tarnished and the UK Parliament became a discredited brand. The UK Parliament is referred to globally as the 'Mother of all Parliaments'. It was one of the first parliaments and many countries have modelled their own government on its format. The word 'parliament' is derived from the French word *parler* which literally means 'to talk'. The UK public expect their politicians to speak the truth and are tired of 'spin'. The general public did not expect to pay for duck houses and moats. Many MPs stood down in disgrace at the following general election and most politicians admitted that they were going to have to work hard to regain the trust of the UK electorate.

Banks
Following the support of the UK government to rescue failing bank brands there was dismay from the public when it was revealed that bonuses were still being paid to employees of the Royal Bank

of Scotland (RBS) and Halifax Bank of Scotland (HBOS). Many banks were unable to lend money to struggling businesses during the 2009 recession and the British public were finding it hard to remortgage their homes; this was not what was expected from our high street banks. RBS and HBOS were receiving large amounts of taxpayers' money, but a limited amount of this money was being distributed to businesses that desperately needed it.

In 2009, Interbrand's annual survey of brands revealed that the main losers in the world's most valuable brands were the banks and financial institutions. The biggest fall was UBS with its brand value halved to $4.4 billion.

There are many examples of big brands behaving unexpectedly. In the Enron scandal of 2001, billions of dollars of debt were hidden from investors. Enron featured a logo that was created by one of America's most celebrated graphic designers, Paul Rand. He designed the corporate logos for some of the world's biggest brands including: IBM, UPS and ABC. The Enron logo features an outline capital 'E' balanced on its heel. It is an elegant piece of graphic design but following the scandal the logo's jaunty angle led to its infamy as the 'crooked E'. The logo inspired the name of a 'made-for-television' film called *The Crooked E – The Unshredded Truth about Enron* (2003).

It is inevitable that every organization will encounter some sort of crisis. Every growing brand will have the occasional growing pains. A crisis is the test of a brand's integrity, but if handled correctly it can help to build the brand.

Innocent

Innocent is an ethical drinks brand selling fresh fruit juice smoothies that are free of preservatives. The founders; Richard Reed, Adam Balon and Jon Wright all met at university. The three friends experimented with various business ventures before they launched Innocent in 1999. Their inspiration came from the morning commute to work. In the late 1990s fresh fruit juice bars were gaining popularity but there were few off-the-shelf options for people in a hurry. Richard, Adam and Jon began by making their own smoothies at home and developed some recipes. The initial market research happened in 1998 at an open-air music festival. They set up a smoothie stall and asked customers to vote on their future by throwing the empty drinks bottles in one of two bins, marked 'yes' or 'no'.

The new business partners wanted to create a brand they could be proud of. After briefly calling the venture 'Fast Tractor', the name 'Innocent' was chosen, summing up the product perfectly but adding a cheeky twist. The Innocent visual identity features a fruit with eyes that is crowned by a halo and goes by the name of 'the dude'. Even the delivery vehicles have charm. The DGVs (Dancing Grass Vans) are ice cream vans covered in artificial grass with cow print seat covers.

The first test for the brand's credibility came in May 2007. The healthy product with an irreverent attitude had made many admirers but this also meant that consumers were playing closer attention to the business. In 2007, Innocent went into partnership with McDonald's and sold children's smoothies in Happy Meals. Innocent's fans expressed their feelings online and complained that the association would compromise Innocent's values. Innocent survived the test and continued to grow.

The second test for the brand came in April 2009 when they sold 20 per cent of their business to Coca-Cola, a brand that isn't famous for its natural health-giving attributes. The transition was an interesting test for the brand.

Innocent have made a real effort in explaining their decision to their customers. The founders published an open letter on their website to explain their decision. It was supplemented with video clips of the founders answering questions about their choice. By being so open and honest about their reasons, they eased the transition and managed to take their customers with them on their journey to expansion. A year later, Coca-Cola

(Contd)

increased their Innocent stake to 58 per cent. Adam, Jon and Richard have retained operational control, working full time at the company. The co-founders published an online update: 'We're excited about this next chapter for Innocent. Simply put, it will help us do more of what we're here to do – get natural, healthy food and drink to as many people as possible.' Innocent have successfully addressed the concerns and expectations of their customers.

Consumers demand transparency. They do not want to be fooled. Business people are expected to justify their decisions to investors. The future of brands depends on honesty and integrity. A brand has to 'do the right thing' if it is to capture the heart of the consumer.

Who owns the brand?

Large corporations with a portfolio of brands employ 'Brand Managers', but once a brand is in the public domain it can start to have a life of its own. You can legally own a brand trade mark, but you cannot control what happens to the brand perception. Sometimes, no matter how hard a brand may strive towards a sophisticated and exclusive image, a celebrity or a social group can still propel it into a different direction.

Burberry is a British luxury goods brand with two royal warrants and a history dating back to 1856. In 2004, the *Eastenders* actress Daniella Westbrook was photographed with her daughter in head to toe Burberry check with a matching handbag and pushchair. *The Sun* newspaper crowned Westbrook the Queen of Chav and later ranked the Burberry incident as its top fashion *faux pas* of the last 50 years. Burberry's signature check pattern acquired the unfortunate nickname of 'Chav Check'. Suddenly the pattern was everywhere, reproduced on baseball caps and draped across teenagers in shopping precincts across the country. The brand was being pushed in a direction that its management could never have planned. Since then, the fashion house has worked hard to reposition itself and in September 2009 it was heralded as a sparkling triumph at its spring/summer fashion show for London Fashion Week. The brand has a new face: the *Harry Potter* actress Emma Watson. Anna Wintour, Editor-in-Chief of *Vogue* said, 'This is a great night for London'. Christopher Bailey, from Yorkshire, is the brand's Creative Director and is responsible for the overall image, advertising and store design. The national media have credited him with turning the brand from a dowdy old label into one of the world's most popular luxury labels. When a brand is compromised by recession, negative publicity or lack of interest it must strive for relevance in people's lives. Innovation and creativity are the priceless assets of brand sustainability.

TEST YOURSELF

▶ *What is a brand?*

▶ *How are you influenced by brands?*

▶ *What's your favourite brand and why?*

▶ *Describe your favourite brand's reputation, experience and expectation.*

▶ *Have you ever lost faith in a brand and if so why?*

▶ *Can you describe the brand architecture of your favourite brand?*

2

Why do I need a brand?

In this chapter you will learn about:
- *differentiation*
- *connecting with people*
- *added value*
- *signifying change*

The way you present yourself, your business, product or service creates an impression, and that impression is your brand. It's the personification of your business and it has an impact on your success. You can't avoid having a brand, so why not make it work to your advantage?

The benefits of creating a brand include:

▶ **Differentiation:** *Branding highlights the differences that make a product or service better than anyone else's.*
▶ **Connecting with people:** *Branding creates a bond between the brand and the consumer that leads to loyalty.*
▶ **Added value:** *Brands create value by adding an emotional significance that exceeds the basic value of the product or service.*
▶ **Signifying change:** *The launch of a brand is an effective way to communicate change in an organization.*

Differentiation

Branding makes it clear to the consumer why a product is better than any other on offer. Price will become the only distinction when you are unable to tell the difference between any two products. It clarifies your market position and what you stand for.

In a competitive market where there is little to choose between two businesses, it's the small details that make the difference. Doing things differently can create rewarding and memorable experiences. What can you recall about your favourite brands?

You don't get a second chance to make a first impression, so the saying goes, and you only have seconds to make a favourable connection. The power of the first impression covers every manifestation of the brand from the shop window to the packaging and advertising – presentation is king. If your website is not clear and intuitive, potential customers will not bother to investigate further.

Malcolm Gladwell, author of the international bestseller *Blink: The Power of Thinking Without Thinking*, writes that snap decisions and first impressions can offer a better means of making sense of the world. Decisions made in two seconds can be every bit as good as decisions made cautiously and deliberately. The conclusion is that first impressions really do count. A brand may be judged in the blink of an eye!

IKEA

Anyone who has wrestled with a self-assembly 'Billy' book case will not forget the experience. But this evergreen item is now 30 years old and proving just as popular with a series of limited editions. Ingvar Kamprad formed Ikea in 1943. The furniture and homeware store offers a complete range of items to make or transform a home – all designed with a Scandinavian influence of simplicity. The store makes great design affordable and accessible.

Ikea is full of memorable experiences that distinguish it from other retailers. Customers collect a giant yellow bag and follow a pre-determined route through the building and will pass products with unusual names like Basisk and Kvart. You can even dine there on their famous meatballs. The store has its critics and fans in equal measure, but it succeeds in delivering a memorable and unique experience. And who hasn't taken home a little wooden pencil with IKEA written on it (thoughtfully provided for list making)?

Soho House

Soho House in London's Greek Street opened 15 years ago. Founder, Nick Jones, told *The Daily Telegraph's* Celia Walden how, 'members' clubs were for men in pinstripe suits who liked to drink port after lunch ... there was a gap in the market for creative, like-minded people. It was born out of reaction to the pomposity of the traditional private members' club – a place where creative types could let their hair down.' In a crowded marketplace, daring to be different can make all the difference.

Insight

Dare to be different! Rise above the competition to be something special. If you are a start-up business without offices, think about an interesting venue to host a meeting that complements your brand, for example, a new hotel, a museum or even an automotive brand experience centre like Mercedes-Benz World at Brooklands (Surrey).

Branding distinguishes your offer from your market competitors by emphasizing the benefits and advantages. Successful branding raises the profile of an ordinary product, service or organization to something special, unique and extraordinary.

Brands create an emotional link in the minds of consumers that help to guide their choices.

Connecting with people

Brands connect with people, culturally, economically and emotionally. A strong brand will earn customer loyalty. The rap band Run DMC declared their love for their favourite brand of training shoes with the rap 'My Adidas', and there is a long tradition of musicians writing songs about car brands, including Prince with 'Little Red Corvette'.

Delia Smith

Brands that connect with people yield great influence. Delia Smith, the popular cook, is a household name and brand in her own right. Delia Smith's cookery books and television shows cause a rush for cooking ingredients and kitchenware. 'Doing a Delia' has its own entry in the *Collins English Dictionary*. It's the first time in the 100-year history of the dictionary that a name has been treated as a brand; it includes separate listings for her name, 'Delia power' and 'a Delia dish'. The Delia effect illustrates the power that brands have in connecting with people and influencing behaviour.

Customer loyalty is the lifeblood of a brand. Loyalty means repeat business. People build loyalties to all types of products or services and swear by them, from cars, clothes, even medicines. In all aspects of life we will encounter a trusted brand.

A survey published in 2009 (by www.thebabywebsite.com) asked 3,000 mums which famous brands they wouldn't give up. The top ten household brands were as follows:

1 *Heinz Tomato Ketchup*
2 *Heinz Baked Beans*
3 *Cadbury's Chocolate*
4 *Walkers Crisps*
5 *Coca-Cola*
6 *Fairy Washing Up Liquid*
7 *Heinz Tomato Soup*

8 *Kellogg's Cornflakes*
9 *Nescafé Coffee*
10 *Hellmann's Mayonnaise*

In a year marked by recession, most of these brands would have had cheaper own-label alternatives. Despite the credit crunch, 52 per cent of mums will not give up their favourite branded products. These results indicate that consumers value quality, reliability and familiarity.

Loyalty can help to build a brand's reputation through word of mouth. Loyal customers become the brand's best advertisement and their enthusiasm can influence the behaviour of friends and associates.

Fans of the Apple computer brand travel great distances to attend the opening of new stores. The store opening becomes a social occasion for other brand fans to meet and share their enthusiasm for the brand.

Harley-Davidson Motorcycles

Can you imagine loving a brand so much that you would tattoo its logo onto your skin? Harley-Davidson owners are so loyal to their favourite motorcycle brand that they make it a lifestyle. The Harley Owners Group® has over one million members worldwide. A whole range of branded clothing is available and many enthusiasts customize their jackets with the iconic logo.

When you've got a loyal following, like Harley-Davidson, your customers sell the product for you. The Harley-Davidson motorcycle brand began in 1903, with William Harley and Arthur Davidson. They supplied motorcycles to the US army in both world wars and the US police forces.

Harley-Davidson has a very strong loyal family that unites people deeply, passionately and authentically, and as such is one of the strongest global brands.

Pizza Express

Pizza Express is a great value family restaurant that makes children feel special – and that's always good for parents! The children have their own three-course menu to choose from, and can finish their meal with a 'Bambinoccino'. They are provided with an activity sheet and coloured pencils to help entertain them. It's these details that differentiate the restaurant chain from other pizza restaurants and means families with young children will remember the meal for the right reasons.

Added value

In the designer handbag market, the profit margins can be ten to twelve times the cost of the bag. Designer handbags are so popular that the phrase 'Baganomics' has been used to describe the trend. In the first decade of this century, British women were spending £350 million on handbags (BBC2, *History of Now: The Story of the Noughties*).

Dana Thomas, author of the book *Deluxe*, said that the marketing departments of luxury brands 'decided that the one thing they had to sell was the heritage of the company, the logo or the brand. The handbag was logoed and instantly recognizable and that was seized on.' The handbag was transformed into a high-visibility advert for luxury brands.

Nilgin Yusuf from the London College of Fashion said, 'It's buying into a dream, an aspiration. It's the bag that you wear to say I've arrived, I'm here and I'm worth something.' Brands create value by adding an emotional significance that exceeds their basic value.

Crème de la Mer

Crème de la Mer is a luxury moisturizing cream. The retail price in July 2010 of a 60 ml pot is £163. Cosmetic and toiletry products are required under European Law to display a full list of ingredients, in descending order of weight. A cosmetic chemist calculated that he could recreate an unbranded 100 ml copycat cream from available ingredients for £9.71.

The Crème de la Mer brand's global president, Maureen Case, explained to *The Daily Mail's* Claire Coleman that they use superior ingredients and the price reflects not just the raw materials but also the costs of helping maintain the ecosystem from which the sea kelp comes by sustainable harvesting. Customers will pay more for exclusivity and a brand that they believe in.

As with house prices, it's what people are prepared to pay. The cost of building a house may only be £100,000, but the sale value can be many times this. It's not just about the building materials, it's about the location, style and what it means to you.

There is a popular saying in business that 'nobody was ever fired for choosing IBM'. IBM is a leading brand in the worldwide server systems market. Investing in technology is an important and expensive decision that most organizations take. Do you risk opting for an unbranded or untried product or choose the company you are familiar with? A brand name adds value by reducing risk to the consumer.

Insight

Legend has it that Picasso once drew a portrait of a woman. She was shocked when he told her it would cost her $5,000. She said, 'but it only took you five seconds to draw,' to which he replied, 'Madame, it took me my entire life'.

Whenever you walk into a Starbucks coffee shop you know what to expect. The colour scheme, furniture and welcoming ambience are a familiar environment to sit and drink coffee with your friends. By having a standard, it becomes easier to manage and implement, reducing your marketing costs. Instead of having to reinvent the wheel each time you want a new shop fit, brochure or van, you will have a set style. The benefits are true for any business at any level, whether it's standardizing the packaging, brochures or business cards. It's about knowing who you are, what you do and how you do it.

When a brand is created it is advisable to write guidelines for its consistent implementation. These should cover all aspects of branded communication and provide templates and standards to follow. A clear set of guidelines will prove their worth by saving you time and money.

Signifying change

An organization may consider a new branding programme when a significant change has happened. This could be change of ownership, change of direction or change of market, the launch of a new product or a start-up business.

Change of image: A refreshed brand image stays true to the brand's ethos but aligns its visual presentation to contemporary tastes. The energy and petrochemicals group Shell is a high street example. The yellow colour and iconic clam shell have remained constant elements throughout their history, but the depiction has become stylized to remain contemporary.

Change of name: In 1999, Procter & Gamble decided to unify the Olay brand under a global name. Previously the brand had been marketed as Oil of Ulay to the UK public.

Change of emphasis: Kentucky Fried Chicken changed its name to KFC, as it no longer wanted to be associated with the word 'fried' and an unhealthy diet. 'We are dramatically changing our menu, our restaurants and the way customers think of us,' said KFC Senior Marketing Vice President Bill McDonald in a prepared statement, 'and we wanted our graphics to reflect the new KFC'.

Change of market: British Petroleum became BP in 2000. The tagline is 'Beyond Petroleum' which eliminates the word 'British' and allows the company to include other types of energy than oil and gas. 'Our brand is summed up by the phrase "beyond petroleum". BP recognizes that meeting the energy challenges of today and tomorrow requires both traditional hydrocarbons and a growing range of alternatives. We are at the forefront of delivering diverse, material and real solutions to meet the world's needs for more and secure, cleaner and affordable energy.'

Following the oil disaster in the Gulf of Mexico in April 2010, the BP brand is under intense scrutiny.

Insight

Many start-ups choose to re-brand after initial success. This often marks a change from their original direction or the expansion of the management team. The branding process is a powerful team-building exercise and will result in a clear vision.

Branding distinguishes your offer from your market competitors by emphasizing the benefits and advantages. A successful brand raises the profile of a product, service or organization to something special, unique and extraordinary. Brands create an emotional link in the mind that helps to guide consumer choice.

TEST YOURSELF

▶ *How do you make a favourable impression?*

▶ *Do you have a consistent brand idea running through your business?*

▶ *Is your company brand memorable, does it stand out from the crowd?*

▶ *Why do your customers keep returning to your business?*

▶ *How would your customers and clients describe your business?*

▶ *In what way can you make your customer experience different from the rest of the market?*

3

Brands in a recession

In this chapter you will learn about:
- **brand-building in a recession**
- **recession disasters**
- **building trust**
- **being relevant**
- **thinking differently**
- **being innovative**
- **the importance of people**

Brand building in a recession

In times of economic recession, the first instinct for many businesses is to cut spending, and the marketing budgets are usually the first to go. But a recession can prove to be the right time to build a brand and there are many examples of famous brands that have started this way.

Sir Richard Branson believes that the next generation of self-made billionaires will appear from the 2008/09 recession. He said to *The Times*' David Robertson, 'Fortunes are made out of recessions. A lot of entrepreneurs get going in the economic depths because the barriers to entry are lower.' The entrepreneur, who got into business at the age of 15, added, 'I've seen four recessions, so I'm quite used to weathering these storms.'

James Caan, entrepreneur and panelist on BBC's *Dragons' Den* said to Sarah Pennells of BBC News 'There is no ideal time to have a great business idea'. He started a headhunting company in 1992 during a UK recession and it proved to be one of his most successful businesses. 'If you've got a good idea today, I think you should go for it. If you truly believe that the idea is a compelling proposition, it's going to work regardless. It may not be as big, it may not grow as fast but it will succeed, because good ideas always work.'

A recession can be the perfect school for an entrepreneur launching a new business brand. The lessons that will be learnt from launching a brand in a recession include:

▶ **Resourcefulness:** *When funds are scarce, you need to think creatively and focus on what is essential.*
▶ **Judgement:** *When the stakes are high, it's paramount that the need for any new product or service is carefully evaluated.*
▶ **Commitment:** *Start-up businesses depend on people who are committed to a shared vision and thrive under pressure.*
▶ **Timing:** *A business that starts in a recession will be in pole position when the market returns.*
▶ **Tenacity:** *When the going gets tough … the tough get going. A recession can reveal winning qualities.*

Brands that started in an economic downturn

Walt Disney	Entertainment	1923
Penguin	Book Publishing	1935
Hewlett-Packard	Technology	1939
Microsoft	Computer Software	1975
Specsavers	Opticians	1984
Sage	Accounting Software	1981
Green & Blacks	Chocolate	1991
FedEx	Courier	1973
MTV	Television Network	1981

Recession disasters

The 2008/09 recession took its toll on public confidence. The reputations of respected banking brands were left in tatters. Northern Rock was nationalized in February 2008 after the first run on a UK bank in more than a century. Following a disastrous merger between Lloyds TSB and Halifax Bank of Scotland (HBOS) the government stepped in and the taxpayer now owns a 43 per cent stake. The government also owns 84 per cent of the Royal Bank of Scotland (RBS). In Iceland the banking system spectacularly collapsed, and in September 2008 Lehman Brothers closed its doors for the last time. It was the biggest bankruptcy in US history and ended Lehman's 158-year reign.

The collapse of these giant banking brands has created a deeply critical view of banking practices and the profession has been tarnished. A public call for transparency and honesty has swept through all areas of business. Perks, freebies or bonuses are considered off-message for most brands.

The global credit crunch has proved a winning source of inspiration for **Steve Knightley and Phil Beer**. The acoustic roots duo who perform under the name 'Show of Hands' won 'Best Original Song' at the 2010 BBC Radio 2 Folk Awards. Their song 'AIG – Arrogance, Ignorance and Greed' criticizes greedy bankers and politicians. Its success registers the public's loss of faith in global banking brands and their damaged reputation.

It wasn't just the banks that suffered; the UK's high street lost two famous retail brands: Woolworths and MFI.

MFI was criticized for poor customer service and its brand name left it open to ridicule: MFI was translated by the general public as 'Made For Idiots'. MFI's dated approach to retail did not compare favourably with competitors like IKEA, who had reinvented the home furnishings market with a completely different way of selling furniture – a help-yourself environment, flat-pack home assembly and clean contemporary designs.

Woolworths is a fondly remembered brand where many music lovers bought their first 7-inch single. At one time, music sales from Woolworths had an impact on the Top 10 music chart, but unfortunately it ceased to be relevant to modern consumer habits with the rise of downloadable music. Woolworths became a last resort destination, as many of the products they offered were available at large supermarkets and hypermarkets that began selling everything from food to clothes and electrical equipment. With out-of-town locations and easy parking it became easier for shoppers to buy everything in one convenient place. The retailer made 90 per cent of its profits in the Christmas period and for the rest of the year just broke even.

Frank Winfield Woolworth founded the first Woolworths in America in 1878, and the store came to England in 1909 selling products at fixed prices of thruppence and a sixpence. The number of stores in the UK would eventually reach 1,000. When F.W. Woolworth died in 1919, his obituary read, 'He won a fortune, not showing how little could be sold for much, but how much could be sold for little.' Woolworths began life as a bargain store and ironically it is the pound shops that are now flourishing.

> **At one time Woolworths was a big music retailer – it was instrumental to the Beatles' success – but supermarkets and the internet took a big slice of the market, and it didn't do enough to preserve that legacy. It kept doing the same old things, like selling penny sweets. It's so hard to build a brand like that – it was bigger than Virgin as a brand, and now it's gone.**
>
> Duncan Bannatyne, OBE, entrepreneur and panellist on BBC's
> *Dragons' Den* (*Mail on Sunday, Live Magazine*),

During the same period a number of other high-profile retail brands went into administration. Brand recognition is so highly valued that investors will snap up the bargains so quickly that the general public are often unaware.

Coffee Republic

The London-based property investor Arab Investments bought the Coffee Republic brand out of administration. Khalid Affara of Arab Investments, said: 'Coffee Republic has a very strong brand name and we are bringing additional investment into the company to expand the number of retail outlets in the UK and elsewhere.'

Readers' Digest

Reader's Digest has been bought out of administration in the UK by a private equity vehicle owned by Jon Moulton. Mark Aldridge, CEO of Better Capital, said: 'It's rare to have an opportunity to back a dynamic management team to run a business with the heritage and brand strength of Reader's Digest.'

Brand survival in a recession

What are the winning qualities for surviving a recession? How do you emerge with your brand in good health? We look at the attributes displayed by some of the strongest brands during times of recession:

- **Trust:** *A recession affects consumer confidence. A proven track record will pay dividends. New enterprises will need to work hard for credibility. Do what you say and be consistent – loyalty is born of trust.*
- **Relevance:** *Is your brand relevant today? Are you offering value, convenience or wellbeing? In a recession, consumers and businesses will take more care in justifying their expenses.*
- **Difference:** *Think different – celebrate the difference that makes you stand apart from your market competitors. Clarity and focus – be clear about what makes you special and what it means to your customers.*

- ▶ **Innovation:** *Create demand – giving people what they didn't know they needed but cannot imagine ever having lived without. New products, services and brands can stimulate demand and get people spending.*
- ▶ **People:** *Invest in people – a positive spirit of fellowship and common purpose among employees is essential in communicating brand confidence. Positive employees make positive customers.*

Trust

A recession will make most people nervous about their job security. The collapse of Lehman Brothers and the government rescue of Northern Rock left the UK's public concerned about the safety of their finances. Shoppers are naturally cautious about spending in a recession. It takes trust to regain consumer confidence.

According to a World Economic Forum (WEF) opinion poll, 130,000 Facebook members from ten G20 economies were asked to choose which values were essential for the global political and economic system. Almost 40 per cent chose 'honesty, integrity and transparency'.

In 2009, the Hovis boy got back on his bike and the Milkybar kid returned to the saddle. Household brands have been capitalizing on their heritage to reassure cash-strapped consumers. Reminding the public of Hovis's 120 years of heritage resulted in an annual sales increase of 13 per cent.

Unilever, owners of the Persil brand, have adopted a similar strategy. The 'Persil mum' features in a montage of advertisements spanning 50 years to remind us that they are a brand to be trusted.

The key to the popularity of these durable advertising campaigns is that they engage the audience and unlock good memories.

In a recession, an inexpensive treat can have a great feel good factor. Consumers demand proven and trusted brands.

In a recession, shoppers don't always buy cheaper brands; they buy fewer premium ones. In 2009, Heinz re-launched the 'Heinz Meanz Beanz' campaign. The baked beans brand predicted that shoppers might be tempted to buy cheaper supermarket alternatives, so they asserted their brand with a familiar campaign. This type of nostalgia works for older brands because it takes shoppers back to carefree days.

Lego

Sales of the iconic building brick brand Lego reached an all-time high during the recession. The Danish brand boasted a 51 per cent increase in UK sales in 2008. Parents have turned to classic brands during the recession. This has boosted the Lego brand position as the UK's third biggest toymaker.

Lego's MD (UK) Marko Ilincic said on Sky News: 'When there are recessions in the UK market, consumers tend to gravitate towards trusted brands ... It's almost as if they can't afford to get it wrong ... I think that's partly the reason why last year, we had a very successful year, as people went back to brands that they trust.'

The brand remains relevant today and continues to engage children with licensed brand themes including Star Wars, Batman and Indiana Jones action adventure sets. The Star Wars line is now in its tenth year and is one of Lego's bestselling ranges.

Marko Ilincic said, 'These are brands and products that have been around for years and keep reinventing themselves.'

Gary Grant, chairman of the Toy Retailers Association, told *The Guardian's* Zoe Wood: 'It has been an outstanding success as parents call on old favourites in hard times. There is an industry-wide shortage of Lego.'

(Contd)

Facts:

▶ *19 billion Lego bricks are produced each year (36,000 per minute)*
▶ *Lego celebrated its 50th anniversary in 2008*
▶ *There are 62 Lego bricks for every person in the world*
▶ *Lego claims that children across the globe spend 5 billion hours a year playing with its Lego bricks.*

The Lego Book, Daniel Lipkowitz

Marks & Spencer

Marks & Spencer (M&S) launched its 125th birthday celebrations in May 2009 by offering a range of M&S products for just one penny. This was a symbolic return to its origins as a Penny Bazaar at the Kirkgate Market in Leeds, where Michael Marks began the business in 1884.

Sir Stuart Rose said in a press release: 'M&S has now been at the heart of Britain for 125 years and we believe that this is something worth celebrating. It's been a tough year for us all but people are fed up with being fed up and we wanted to give our customers a real treat.' Their continuing ethos is promoted on their website: 'Our company values of Quality, Value, Service, Innovation and Trust are not new – they are the principles on which our business was founded in 1884'. To tie in with the anniversary, M&S have released a range of clothing and accessories inspired by their archive. The heritage campaign created extra publicity with celebrity appearances by the 1960s model Twiggy and the launch of a book charting the store's history.

Relevance

A relevant brand stands for something that connects with the consumer and is applicable to their lives.

When Chris Evans, the radio presenter, appeared on BBC's *The Andrew Marr Show* (10 January 2010) he said that his new Radio 2 breakfast slot would be 'mostly music – but listeners want warmth, wit and relevance'. He had big shoes to replace following the retirement of Terry Wogan. He appears to have succeeded and listener figures are building since his debut in January 2010.

So what has 'relevance' to do with branding in a recession? To succeed in a depressed market, when consumers have little spare cash and are stretched for free time, a brand must demonstrate significance to their lifestyle and value for money.

Travelodge

The 2009 recession saw a boom in UK holiday destinations as the British public chose to relax closer to home and take a 'staycation'. Grant Hearn, Chief Executive of Travelodge said, 'Despite a very challenging market, we have chosen to invest and grow throughout the recession. Consumers have chosen low-cost, quality accommodation rather than overpriced full-service and mid-market establishments.' He also attributed their popularity to businesses trying to lower their travel costs.

Travelodge is number two in its sector after the Whitbread Premier Inn chain. At the beginning of 2010, Travelodge was operating 390 hotels across the UK, Ireland and Spain, and employing 5,500 people. Travelodge now plans to grow by opening 26 new hotels in 2010. This will create 500 new jobs across the country, with an investment of £115 million. Grant Hearn commented on *Jeff Randall Live* – Sky News, 'Back in 1990 only one in five people stayed in a hotel in this country; that number is now one in three and that is totally down to the growth of branded budget hotels.'

Difference

'The ones who see things differently. They're not fond of rules. And they have no respect for the status quo. You can praise them, disagree with them, quote them, disbelieve them, glorify or vilify them. About the only thing you can't do is ignore them.' These words formed part of the dialogue for 'Apple Computers Think Different' campaign. The copy is written in the style of Jack Kerouac's iconic book, *On the Road*. It celebrates how thinking differently can be a benefit to society, and it works for brands too.

Apple

Thinking differently was a deciding factor in Apple's recovery from financial difficulty. In 1996 the Apple brand had lost its healthy glow. The range of products was less than inspiring and the leadership lacked charisma. On 14 June 1997, Steve Jobs returned to the business he had founded. He restructured the product range and started developing a network computer that would evolve into the iMac. In 1984, Apple had run a very successful advert by Advertising Agency Chiat/Day. The campaign was based on George Orwell's *1984* and was directed by Ridley Scott. In dramatic style it set the Apple brand apart from its competitors, creating an 'us and them' perspective. A similar tactic was required to put Apple's brand back into consumers' minds. The 1997 campaign was also created by Chiat/Day, and featured black and white portraits of famous people. These included: Albert Einstein, Richard Branson, Muhammad Ali, Mahatma Gandhi, Amelia Earhart and Pablo Picasso. Living participants and the estates of the deceased were given computer equipment and money for donation to non-profit organizations and charities. Instead of placing the adverts in trade and computer retail magazines they appeared in the mainstream popular press. The campaign was launched on 28 September 1997 and was a big success and a turning point for Apple. The 'Think different' campaign ran until 2002.

Aldi

How can you be different in the fiercely competitive world of supermarket chains? Aldi has found a niche. In the recession of 2009, the German supermarket chain won numerous industry awards, including *Which?* 'Best Supermarket 2009' and *The Grocer* 'The Grocer of the Year 2009'. Aldi sell their products under their own label names, and the in-store displays are functional and devoid of flashy point of sale distractions. They narrow consumer choice by offering less variety in each category. Aldi was the most successful supermarket group over the Christmas period 2008. The store appears to be attracting well-healed clientele. Paul Foley, Managing Director of Aldi UK, said to Harry Wallop of *The Daily Telegraph*, 'Consumers are trying something new, but it is also the style and the quality of the offer that is attractive.'

Innovation

To be No 1 you have to act like you are No 2 ... and be daring, innovative and creative.

John Perkins, Managing Director of Specsavers
speaking to Andrew Davidson, *The Sunday Times*

Innovation transforms ideas into inspiring products and services, leaping to a completely new and different way of doing things.

Gym memberships are usually the first thing to be cancelled when times are hard, but entertainment and fitness are key to a sense of wellbeing. Adults are recommended to take at least 30 minutes of exercise, at least five times a week to stay fit. The innovation of one company led to an endorsement by the NHS:

Nintendo

Nintendo is a Japanese pioneer of interactive entertainment. The company from Kyoto is the brand behind the fastest selling console of all time: the Wii was launched in 2006 and by 2009 it had shipped a record-breaking 50 million units. The company reported that in a year of global recession its profits were the strongest to date. The Wii is unlike other consoles in that it depends on physical movement and provides a unique interactive

(Contd)

experience. Exercise programmes and activities on the system have been judged to be as beneficial as 'real world' exercise. A balance board can be used with the system that enables skiing practice and aerobics. The National Institute of Health and Nutrition in Tokyo conducted research and found that Wii Sport Boxing was as beneficial as a round of golf carrying your own clubs.

A spokesperson for the Department of Health endorsed the console: 'Activity like this throughout the day can easily add up to the 60 active minutes that children need or the 30 minutes that adults need five times a week.'

Its successful products include Nintendo DS and Nintendo DSi, and the older Game Boy. It has also created entertainment icons that have become household names including; Mario, Donkey Kong, Metroid, Zelda and Pokémon.

Genius is 99 per cent perspiration and 1 per cent inspiration.

Thomas Edison, inventor of the light bulb

People

A survey by Gallup has found that the key to an enduring customer relationship is 'customer facing employees'. It is the employees who represent the brand to customers. In a service-based business, it is the staff who are tested to realize the brand promise.

Jackie Orme, Chief Executive of the Chartered Institute of Personnel and Development (CIPD) says, 'Firms that have built trust and engagement and a firm sense of common purpose over time are reaping the rewards in terms of motivated employees willing to go the extra mile, despite the tough environment.'

The CIPD sponsors *The Sunday Times* 'Best Companies to Work For' survey. Employee satisfaction is not just for the good times.

The stresses and pay freezes of a recession take their toll on employee morale. The survey judges company performance on eight factors: Leadership, Wellbeing, My Manager, My Team, Fair Deal, Giving Something Back, My Company and Personal Growth.

Nando's Restaurants

Nando's has a chain of 220 restaurants in the UK. The brand specializes in chicken with a Portuguese theme. It all started in South Africa in 1987, when the founders, Robbie and Fernando, chose the Barcelos Cockerel of Portugal as their company symbol because it stood for faith, justice and goodluck.

Nando's 6,300 employees are known as 'Nandocas'. Together they have helped to rank the business as the best big company to work for in the UK. What makes Nando's employees so happy? Human resources director Julia Claydon says, 'The principle philosophy is creating a different kind of place to work. We wanted people to enjoy their jobs and it has been that way from the beginning.'

Nando's employees love working for the brand and enjoy a strong sense of team spirit. The restaurant values individuals and 'Nandocas' feel able to speak openly with their managers. Each employee is eligible for 45 hours of training annually and in some circumstances have had time off and tuition fees paid for full-time studying. Maternity arrangements are generous and working hours are very flexible.

Happy staff are essential for a brand that depends on good customer service.

Insight

Set the highest standard you can and make sure it's consistent and sustainable.

TEST YOURSELF

► *Why do consumers trust your brand?*

► *How is your brand relevant?*

► *How are you different?*

► *How is your brand innovative?*

► *How do you invest in your people?*

4

Brand value

In this chapter you will learn about:
- *reasons for calculating brand value*
- *brands and investors*
- *intangible assets*
- *what brand valuation is*
- *financial methods to value a brand*
- *brand valuation reports*
- *overvalued brands*

A brand is a valuable business asset that is taken seriously by accountants and investors. The growth in a brand's value is of interest to finance professionals concerned with increasing shareholder value and marketers focused on increased sales and profit margin.

> **In the past several decades, there has been a dramatic shift, a transformation, in what economists call the production functions of companies – the major assets that create value and growth. Intangibles are fast becoming substitutes for physical assets.**
>
> Baruch Lev, The Philip Bardes Professor of Accounting and Finance at New York University's Leonard N. Stern School of Business

It takes time to build a brand. Acquiring a brand name can be a short cut to success. A strong brand will command a premium price if the brand name is available for purchase. The following examples indicate that even when a business has ceased to trade, the brand name has a distinct and quantifiable value.

Woolworths

The British high street store Woolworths went into administration in December 2008 with debts of £385 million. It was famous for its Pick'n'Mix sweets, Ladybird children's clothes and Chad valley toys. The administrator, Deloitte sold the brand assets to two leading British retail groups:

Shop Direct Group bought the Woolworths brand name and some sub-brands, including Ladybird clothing, for £7 million according to Marcus Leroux at *The Times*. Chief Executive Mark Newton-Jones said: 'We are delighted to be relaunching the Woolworths name online. Woolworths is a much loved brand that engenders huge affection among British consumers and is an important part of the country's retail heritage. In what will be Woolworths' 100th year, we are proud to be reviving the brand for future generations' (DrapersOnline).

Home Retail Group, the owner of Argos and Homebase, bought the Woolworths toy brand Chad Valley for £5m. Argos has a leading position in the toy retail market. The retailer said it had purchased the rights to use the Chad Valley brand exclusively in the UK and internationally. Chad Valley has strong heritage, with high recognition in the UK.

Zavvi

The high street entertainment brand Zavvi went into administration in December 2008 following the collapse of Woolworths, its main supplier. In March 2009 The Hut Group announced its acquisition of the brand. Matthew Moulding, CEO of The Hut Group, said, 'Zavvi is a major player in entertainment retail, both in the UK and Ireland. Our aim is to capitalize on this well recognized high street brand and transform the business into a leading class online retailer, not only in entertainment, but also across lifestyle products.' Acquiring the Zavvi brand has enabled The Hut Group to connect with a wider group of young online shoppers.

Reasons for calculating brand value

The Intellectual Property Office conducted an Awareness Survey in 2006. It revealed that over 96 per cent of small to medium-sized enterprises (SMEs) had never assessed how much their intellectual property was worth. Establishing a brand's value is necessary for:

▶ *brand investment decisions*
▶ *marketing budget allocation*
▶ *communication of brand worth*
▶ *putting a brand on the balance sheet**
▶ *establishing a brand's value for mergers and acquisitions*
▶ *securing finance – some companies put their brand up as collateral.*

*UK companies are only allowed to place acquired brands on the balance sheet, but internally generated brands are not allowed at the present time.

Insight

For information about intellectual assets, including free tools for asset management, visit the Intellectual Assets Centre at http://www.ia-centre.org.uk.

Brands attract investors

Warren Buffett

Warren Buffett is one of the most successful investors in history. In March 2010 Warren Buffett was ranked as the world's third wealthiest person with a fortune of $47 billion in the Forbes List of Billionaires. According to the *Financial Times*, Buffet now considers the brand first when investing in businesses, the management team second and a strong balance sheet third.

Your premium brand had better be delivering something special, or it's not going to get the business.

Warren Buffett

Silver Cross Prams

David Halsall of Halsall Toys International (HTI), bought the Silver Cross brand in 2002. The acquisition took place one month after it had gone into receivership. Alan Halsall, the Joint Managing Director, said: 'Brand names as famous and with such heritage as Silver Cross are extremely rare and we are very excited at the opportunity we now have.' The Silver Cross pram brand can trace its origins back to 1877 when its founder William Wilson produced the first coach-built model at his Yorkshire workshop in Silver Cross Street, Leeds. Members of the royal family have used Silver Cross prams and a pram was given to George VI for Princess Elizabeth. In 2010 the brand has distribution in Asia, the Middle East, North America, Russia and Europe and sells to 30 countries worldwide. The Silver Cross Lifestyle range has won many prestigious awards.

Intangible asset

A brand is an intangible asset. Intangible assets are all forms of knowledge that contribute to your products and services, but don't always have a physical presence. Intangible assets include reputation, brand, skills and knowledge, employee, customer and supplier relationships, goodwill, contracts, domain names, software and processes. They are distinct from tangible assets, which have a physical presence, for example factories, machinery and equipment.

The world's economy is supported by imagination and ideas. Brand Finance, the world's leading independent brand valuation consultancy, completed an extensive global study of intangible value in 2008. It covered over 37,000 businesses, which represented 99 per cent of the world's quoted companies.

The surveyed companies had a total enterprise value (market value for the whole business) of $38.6 trillion, with 40 per cent of the value representing intangible assets.

According to The Intellectual Property Office, most UK businesses' intangible assets are 'the single-most valuable asset class and typically represent well over 50 per cent of corporate value'.

Insight

For general information about valuing intangibles, visit the Business Link website at http://www.businesslink.gov.uk and go to the section 'Identifying, protecting and transferring your assets'.

If this business were to split up, I would be glad to take the brands, trade marks and goodwill and you could have all the bricks and mortar – and I would fare better than you.

John Stuart, former Chairman of Quaker Oats

Norton Motorcycles

Stuart Garner is a Derbyshire based businessman who has invested millions of his own money acquiring the rights to the Norton motorcycle brand. The acquisition in 2008 included all the trade mark rights and development work from its 15 years under American ownership.

Stuart Garner told Andy Downes of MCN, 'We want to take the brand forward in terms of design and engineering. Norton is a fabulous name and we already connect with the guys out there who are in their 40s, 50s, 60s and beyond, because they remember the good days. What we need to do is get into the minds of the people out there who are not aware of Norton and what it's all about.'

Its model names – Dominator, Atlas and Commando – are practically brands in their own right. Norton's past successes

(Contd)

at the Isle of Man TT races are legendary. Stuart Garner has invested in the pedigree of the Norton brand name and the goodwill of a mature community of motorcycle enthusiasts. The test will be in translating the Norton brand values to a new younger audience. Garner said, 'This is the beginning of a new and exciting era in a brand that was started over 100 years ago by James Lansdowne Norton. It has sustained ups and downs over the years but still stands for performance and excellence. These will be the standards we live by from now on.'

Brand valuation definition

There is no standard definition of the word 'brand' and the word is generally used to encompass a wide range of assets. Three different concepts are commonly used to define the word 'brand'. They are as follows:

1 **Trade mark:** *Focuses on the legal protection of verbal and visual elements including, logos, trade names, trade marks and trade symbols.*
2 **The brand:** *A more extensive category including all items in point 1 as well as domain names, product design rights, uniforms, packaging, copyrights, descriptors, sounds, colours, smells, etc.*
3 **Branded business:** *The whole business including all items in points 1 and 2 together with the culture, people and activities.*

(*The International Brand Valuation Manual*,
Gabriela Salinas)

> **Insight**
> Brand Finance's website is useful for information on brand valuation and the latest branding surveys. Visit http://www.brandfinance.com.

Financial methods to value a brand

The world's first valuation standard is planned for release in 2010. The standard ISO/DIS 10668 was developed by the International Organization for Standardization (ISO) with input from the British Standards Institution (BSI) in the UK. The standard will specify the requirement for procedures and methods of monetary brand value measurement. There are 14 participating countries including Germany, Australia, China, France, Japan, Republic of Korea (South Korea), Spain and the United Kingdom.

The three main methods of brand valuation, which will be endorsed by the new standard ISO/DIS 10668 are:

▸ **Income approach:** *Measures the future income which the brand may generate and the costs of generating that income over the economic life of the brand.*
▸ **Market approach:** *Measures the value of the brand based on what other purchasers in the market have paid for similar assets.*
▸ **Cost approach:** *Measures the value of the brand based on the cost invested in it.*

(BSI Press Release, 24 July 2009)

Insight

For an in-depth explanation of brand valuation methods, please refer to the book *Competitive Success* by John A. Davis and *The International Brand Valuation Manual* by Gabriela Salinas.

Brand valuation reports

Brand Finance and Interbrand (the world's largest branding consultancy), both publish high-profile annual reports on global brand valuation. Each company has its own methodology for working out the valuations. Brand Finance publishes the 'Brand Finance Global 500' and Interbrand publish their 'Best Global Brands' report.

Brand valuations can produce widely differing values. To illustrate this, in Interbrand's September 2009 survey, Coca-Cola is their number one brand with a value of $68.7 billion. In Brand Finance's February 2010 survey, Coca-Cola is third with a value of $34.8 billion – a $33.9 billion difference!

Brand valuation can be seen as an art rather than a science. Values are only realized when the brand is sold.

Brands are the largest source of intangible assets yet, historically, brand valuation has been viewed as opaque, subjective and unreliable – a bit of a black art. The ISO standard recognizes this and attempts to create a consensus on how brands should be valued.

David Haigh, CEO Brand Finance

Interbrand's Top 10 Brands	Interbrand Valuation Sept 09 ($Billions)
Coca-Cola	68.7
IBM	60.2
Microsoft	56.6
GE	47.7
Nokia	34.8
McDonald's	32.2
Google	31.9
Toyota	31.3
Intel	30.6
Disney	28.4

Brand Finance Top 10 Brands	Brand Finance Valuation Feb 10 ($Billions)
Wal–Mart	41.3
Google	36.1
Coca-Cola	34.8
IBM	33.7

Brand Finance Top 10 Brands	Brand Finance Valuation Feb 10 ($Billions)
Microsoft	33.6
GE	31.9
Vodafone	28.9
HSBC	28.4
HP	27.3
Toyota	27.3

Brand value examples

Brand Finance's 'Global 500 Results' from February 2010, show that a brand like Estée Lauder can represent up to 67 per cent of the Enterprise value (market value for the whole business).

Estée Lauder is a luxury brand and most observers would expect them to have a high brand value. However, companies like Sainsbury's have a brand value of 50 per cent and business-to business companies like Thales are on 25 per cent. All well-known brands, whatever sector they are in, have a significant value. Companies need to take care of their branded assets if their enterprise value is to remain high!

In February 2010, *The Daily Telegraph's* Graham Ruddick reported that, Brand Finance downgraded Toyota's brand from its AAA rating (extremely strong brand) and a value of $27 billion, to an A rating (strong brand) and worth $24 billion. This 10 per cent reduction was attributed to Toyota's poor handling of the recall of more than 8 million cars.

Brand value as a percentage of enterprise value

	Brand Value/ Enterprise Value	Brand Value 2010 US $billions	Enterprise Value 2010 US $billions
Estée Lauder	67%	2.5	3.8
Nike	64%	15.8	24.7
Avon	61%	9.9	16.1

(Contd)

	Brand Value/ Enterprise Value	Brand Value 2010 US $billions	Enterprise Value 2010 US $billions
Sears	59%	4.2	7.1
Kroger	57%	5.0	8.8
Polo Ralph Lauren	56%	2.9	5.2
Dell	53%	9.7	18.2
Whirlpool	53%	2.4	4.5
Adidas	51%	5.7	11.2
Airbus	50%	2.6	5.2
Sainsbury's	50%	6.3	12.7

Overvalued brands

John Gerzema and Ed Lebar in their 2008 bestselling business book *The Brand Bubble* believe that there is another bubble in the world's economy. 'This bubble represents $4 trillion in Standard & Poor's (S&P) market capitalization alone. It's twice the size of the subprime mortgage market and it accounts for over one-third of all shareholder value.'

Their main concern is that financial markets and investors have overvalued brands. If the bubble were to burst, the intangible value of many companies would be severely reduced, therefore reducing their enterprise value and creating panic in the global economy.

Their conclusion is based on 15 years of brand and financial data from Young & Rubican's BrandAsset® Valuator (BAV), the world's largest study of consumer attitudes and perceptions on brands. They have been measuring brands since 1993 and today over 35,000 brands have been evaluated in 46 countries.

TEST YOURSELF

▶ *Why do companies calculate brand value?*

▶ *What does Warren Buffett look for when investing in a business?*

▶ *What are intangible assets?*

▶ *What percentage of Enterprise Value do intangible assets account for in 99 per cent of the world's quoted companies?*

▶ *What are the three valuation definitions of the word brand?*

▶ *What are the three financial methods of brand valuation?*

5

Brand focus

In this chapter you will learn about:
- *pioneering brands*
- *creative brands*
- *innovative brands*
- *caring brands*
- *communicative brands*
- *knowledgeable brands*
- *inspirational brands*

One thing that great brands share in common is focus. A focused brand has a clear vision of the future that guides the organization on its path to growth. Customers, consumers and clients who connect with that vision will help to strengthen the brand.

We have chosen seven brands that best illustrate the entrepreneurial qualities of Pioneering, Creativity, Innovation, Care, Communication, Knowledge and Inspiration. Each brand has very different characteristics but they all aim to make the world a better place. These brands have chosen paths that are not dictated by financial reward alone. Some have been guided by a desire to improve people's lives and some have changed the world for good.

The following case studies illustrate how great brands add value to their customers' lives as well as returning value to their investors. Behind these brands are visionary thinkers who put their heart into the business. If you create a brand on a hollow promise, the truth will eventually be revealed.

The secret of success is to do the common things uncommonly well.

John D. Rockerfeller

Pioneering

What is a pioneering brand? Pioneers are passionate, fearless and very independent. They are leaders who move the market forward with their ideas; they change the way people think and break through into new territories. They are confident self-starters, courageous, energetic and dynamic. They are determined to succeed where other businesses would give up. These are exciting and brave brands that offer an alternative.

Pioneering is about discovery, being radical and having the energy and determination to move forward. The twentieth century witnessed many pioneers make astonishing discoveries that would usher in commercial opportunities that changed the world forever, from the Wright Brothers, pioneers of aviation, to NASA, making the first moon landing; from John Logie Baird, pioneer of television, to Tim Berners Lee, pioneer of the internet; from James D. Watson and Francis Crick and the discovery of DNA to the mapping of the human genome.

Key words

passion, fearless, independent, first, lead, ideas, start, courageous, energetic, dynamic, determination, perseverance, breakthrough, exciting, enthusiastic, brave, different, create, explore, discover, initiate, instigate, launch, originate, visionary, new.

Virgin

Sir Richard Branson founded Virgin in 1970. The brand started as a mail order record business, and a shop in London's Oxford Street followed a year later. The name Virgin was chosen because he was new to business; other options included 'Slipped Disc'. The success of the record shop led to the next step, setting up a record studio in Oxfordshire called 'The Manor'. The artist Roger Dean, famous for album covers of progressive rock bands including Yes, drew the first Virgin Records label. The design, which featured a serpent and Gemini twins, appeared on advertisements and vinyl. Ray Kyte of Kyte & Company created the familiar red and white signature design that appears today throughout the Virgin Group. Analysts have described the angle of the signature from left to right as upbeat. Branson in his autobiography *Losing My Virginity* described it as his personal endorsement. It is popularly known as the 'Scrawl'.

The Virgin record label was launched in 1973 together with Virgin Music Publishing. The Mike Oldfield album, *Tubular Bells*, was the first Virgin release and became one of the biggest selling albums of the 1970s. The record label pioneered new musical genres and artists including The Sex Pistols and Culture Club.

In 1984, Virgin launched the airline Virgin Atlantic. The industry reaction was sceptical, but Virgin already had a track record for pushing boundaries. Virgin was taking a pioneering step by challenging the established brands of transatlantic flight, in particular British Airways (BA). Humour has never been far from the Virgin brand and in typically irreverent style it started a NO WAY BA/AA campaign against the proposed merger of BA and American Airlines. This positioned the Virgin brand as a people's champion fighting against monopoly and keeping prices down.

The Virgin Group has now expanded into leisure, travel, tourism, mobile phones, broadband, TV, radio, music festivals, finance and health. The Virgin brand name appears on 200 companies in over

30 countries. With the Virgin Green Fund the brand is investing in renewable energy and resource efficiency.

Virgin's style is informal, irreverent, witty and fun. The brand has a number of impressive firsts in its pioneering history:

Virgin Media
▶ *First UK phone provider offering free 'home phone to mobile' call rates for new and existing customers.*

Virgin Atlantic
▶ *First UK airline to order the Boeing 787-9 Dreamliner.*
▶ *First airline to offer individual televisions to business class passengers.*
▶ *First airline to offer interactive entertainment in all classes.*

Virgin Galactic
▶ *First spaceline, giving ordinary people the experience of space travel.*

Virgin Holiday
▶ *Vroom – first airport lounge dedicated to holidaymakers.*

Virgin Festivals
▶ *The V Festival – first festival to be staged in two different locations in one weekend.*

The success of Virgin demonstrates that a brand name does not need to be locked into one group. Some of the Virgin companies, such as Virgin Radio, have been sold, but Branson's personality and the Virgin image are inextricably linked. Virgin is a truly pioneering company, led by a pioneering leader. He embodies this spirit through his own endeavors of breaking world records with balloon flights and fast boats. Now, with Virgin Galactic, the brand is boldly going where no brand has gone before. Space must be 'the final frontier' for a pioneering brand!

Creative

Creativity is often viewed as an add-on for most businesses. But creativity can be the guiding force that helps a business focus on success. All brands begin with an idea. The growth and development of the brand depends on the constant supply of new ideas. Unfortunately, most businesses do not foster this resource or facilitate the generation of ideas. Productivity and performance overshadow everything and stifle the creative process. If a business has a creative or design department it is often given its own space away from the rest of the team. Taking people out of a fixed environment can release new trains of thought. A culture that values creativity can benefit from the abrasive effect of different personalities and disciplines. These businesses are sociable, fun and expressive.

The need to be right all the time is the biggest bar there is to new ideas. It is better to have enough ideas for some of them to be wrong than to be always right by having no ideas at all.

Edward De Bono

Key words

right-brained, creative, instinctive, imaginative, expressive, emotional, confident, happy, enthusiastic, sociable, fun, original, dramatic, elegant, sensitive, sensory, stylish, flexible, intuitive, objective, feelings, lateral, free, transformational, visual.

Apple

Apple has long been the brand of choice for the creative industries; musicians, artists, designers and architects use Apple computers to run the applications of their trade. The brand now has mainstream appeal with the huge success of the iPhone – the must-have mobile. More than just a communications device, the iPhone places creativity in the palm of your hand with limitless opportunities for customization. The iPhone's tactile finish and intuitive interface enables the download of a myriad of applications – known as Apps – to suit the individual. The Apps cover everything from social media, recipes, games and sport.

Apple encourages software developers to create new Apps with its Software Development Kit (SDK) and they have eagerly responded to the invitation. Since launching the App Store in July 2008 with 500 Apps, today there are now more than 150,000 available.

Since 2008 over 3 billion Apps have been downloaded. One of the most popular is 'Brush'. This is a finger painting application that has inspired artists to use the digital medium. It's proved so successful that art created with this application has featured on the front cover of the *New Yorker Magazine*. The artist Jorge Colombo explained that the surprising advantage of using his phone to sketch with was its anonymity. He could sketch in public without raising attention and the backlit surface allows him to work in poor light conditions.

Apple is *the* creative brand because they present exciting new ways of doing things. Suddenly a phone isn't just for making calls, it's a mobile entertainment suite, personal assistant and route finder – Apple has the creative knack for redefining a genre.

Steve Jobs is the charismatic CEO who has captained this route to success. He was a founding partner back in 1976. When he returned to the brand in late 1996, the brand was in trouble. He introduced the iMac and put down a firm foot on the return path to success. The colourful personal computer added style to homes and offices everywhere – beige was dead; colour had finally come to the world of PCs.

(Contd)

They followed the success of the iMac with iTunes, which was a new way of downloading MP3 music. To follow this they created their own MP3 player, the Apple iPod. MP3 players already existed, but this one was different – it had a much longer battery life and had a revolutionary navigation method to give users faster access to their music. iPod has become a generic term and part of the language; other MP3 players are now referred to as iPods – in the same way that vacuum cleaners are called Hoovers. Its success re-energized the Apple brand. Apple have now attracted a new customer base to their products and have maintained the winning streak by creating the Apple iPhone.

Steve Jobs' biography describes him as having 'a bizarre obsession with the insides of his machines'. Engineers are driven mad by his insistence that the insides of Apple machines look beautiful too, even though most people will never see them! Apple's products are different from everyone else's. They are minimalist and stylish, they are intuitive to use and they have personality.

He has the mind of an engineer and the heart of an artist.

Larry Ellison, CEO of Oracle, talking about Steve Jobs
(*Financial Times* 30/31 January 2010)

Jonathan Ive is one of the most important creative figures in recent history and he is responsible for some of the most iconic products since the turn of the millennium. His position at Apple places creativity right at the heart of the brand.

He is Apple's Senior Vice President for Industrial Design. The Englishman's position in the business has been closely linked to its recent successes. His profile can be found next to Steve Jobs in the Executive Profiles section of Apple's website. He has led Apple's design team towards numerous design awards and his products are displayed in the collections of international museums including New York's MOMA and the Pompidou in Paris. His awards include: Design Museum London – Designer of the Year; The Royal Society of Arts – Royal Designer for Industry and he has been honoured with a CBE.

At a ceremony to receive an honorary doctorate from the Royal College of Art (RCA) he revealed some insights into how Apple work. Speaking with the RCA's Rector, Professor Sir Christopher Frayling, he said that Apple do not use focus groups and prefer to go from idea to making a prototype. Ive has a passion for making objects: 'Prototypes create this dramatic shift in the conversation – suddenly it becomes tangible and the silence goes away.' He attributed the brand's success to not being driven by money, but focused on producing desirable and useful objects.

Launch dates of significant products by Jonathan Ive at Apple include:

1998 iMac
1999 Apple iBook
2001 iPod MP3 player and Titanium PowerBook G4
2004 iPod mini and iMac G5 (ultra-slim)
2007 iPhone
2010 iPad

The combined success of the iPod, iPhones and Mac laptops has redefined the Apple brand as the world's number one mobile device brand. Not content to rest on their laurels they continue to change our habits with genre-busting technology. The speculation around the launch of the iPad provoked *The Wall Street Journal*'s comment: 'The last time there was this much excitement about a tablet, it had some commandments written on it.' The iPad was inspired by a desire to bridge the gap between laptops and smart phones. Netbooks are good at nothing, said Jobs at the launch of the iPad; he wanted a product that was better at browsing the web, email, photo albums, videos, music, games and e-books. The iPad uses the same touch screen operability that 75 million people already enjoy with the iTouch and it hooks up with all the iPhone Apps that are available on the Apps Store. Apps developers are enjoying the new opportunities of creating new Apps for a larger screen; it's a thriving environment to release the creative potential of developers. The iPad is much more than an e-book reader and

(Contd)

proves attractive competition for the Kindle by Amazon. The iBook store was launched with cooperation from five major publishers: Penguin, HarperCollins, Simon & Schuster, Macmillan and Hachette Book Group.

Jonathan Ive described the impact of the iPad: 'It defines our vision, our sense of what's next.'

The Apple business recruits people who share their creative ambition. Their website claims to appeal to people 'who are smart, creative, up for any challenge, and incredibly excited about what they do'. The Apps team is described as 'ultra technical yet incredibly creative'. Throughout the organization, creativity is valued and championed, making Apple a very creative brand.

Innovative

Most people are naturally conservative and resistant to change. The job of the innovator is a challenging one. As if the task of inventing something new and useful isn't hard enough, they then need to convince us that we actually needed the device in the first place! It can take time to move public opinion. The stakes are high but the rewards can be huge. The innovator may succeed in creating an entirely new class of product and become the brand leader.

What is an innovative business? It is one that values clear, rational and focused thinking. Being first to market with a new concept can mean the difference between survival and failure. Today, innovation is not the sole preserve of the lonely genius working away at a theory. Whole teams of people share ideas in a cooperative spirit. New products are researched and examined from every perspective. They employ people who are analytical, technical and logical.

left-brained, clear, rational, focused, analytical, technical, logical, reasoned, process, cutting edge, verbal, organized, subjective, persuasive, functional, ingenious, inventive, original, revolutionary, engineered.

Dyson

Sir James Dyson is a designer and entrepreneur. He is best known for his bagless dual cyclone vacuum cleaner. His first commercial success was the ball barrow – a wheelbarrow with a ball instead of a wheel. Latest innovations include hand dryers that use only a sixth of electricity of conventional models and a bladeless fan that provides a constant air flow.

The success of his vacuum cleaner followed years of perseverance perfecting his idea before he had the finished invention. It received 'The International Design' first prize in Japan in 1991.

His innovation has paid off and the vacuum cleaner is still number one by value in the American market. In 2010 the Dyson business is still growing with 2,500 employees and a £628m turnover with £85m profit.

Sir James Dyson is passionate about innovation. In March 2010 he carried out a review, titled 'Ingenious Britain'. He was quoted in the national press saying that 'kids should aspire to be scientists and not models'. He maintains that Britain still has the talent and resources to lead the world in innovation. Dyson is concerned that the UK relies too heavily on the service sector, and in particular, financial services. The UK cannot compete internationally on cost

(Contd)

CASE STUDY

or volume. Innovation takes time. He has warned that China, South Korea and India are now investing in home-grown innovation. The UK must export its technology if it is to stand a chance against international competition. Dyson has appealed for enthusiastic science graduates to take up teaching, to inspire young people. 'We've not invented everything. We never will' (*The Sun*).

He says we must stop financial services siphoning off the best brains. 'They take 50 per cent of engineering graduates.' He also says that, 'The business press concentrates so much on the City that takeovers and salaries start to become the news. If there was more coverage of manufacturing, more children could be inspired to make things. If we invent more, we own more intellectual property, we keep the profits.'

Sir James Dyson is stepping down as CEO and is returning to what he enjoys best – innovating. He wants to spend more time 'working in the labs where the real invention happens' (*The Sunday Times*, 14 March 2010).

The Dyson brand is about making things work better through perseverance, creativity and perfectionism; in short, it's about innovation. Sir James Dyson sees innovation as a driving force for the nation's survival, offering a route out of recession. In 2010 Dyson is recruiting 350 new engineers to work on research and development projects as part of an expansion programme. Dyson is the UK's second biggest filer of patents after Rolls-Royce.

Caring

Brands are interconnected with their employees, suppliers and customers. They are a part of society and can affect the environment or our physical health. Commerce has global implications and with that comes responsibility. Sustainability and Corporate Social Responsibility (CSR) are the two 'must have' policies for global businesses. But is CSR a charity bandwagon or really heart-felt?

Either way, a lot of good causes benefit from these policies, but there is a difference between believing in a cause and just doing the right thing. A hollow CSR policy will come up for scrutiny but passionate heart-felt causes could be the focus that drives a brand. Dame Anita Roddick founded the ethical beauty brand 'The Body Shop' and placed 'Against Animal Testing' on the political agenda. The brand was the first global cosmetics brand to be recognized under the Humane Cosmetics Standard for their 'Against Animal Testing' policy.

The business of business should not just be about money, it should be about responsibility. It should be about public good, not private greed.

Dame Anita Roddick, The Body Shop founder

A caring business brand is one where heart-felt community relationships are built. The brand's growth is guided by a solid insight into society's needs and an awareness of corporate social responsibility. The caring brand is driven by a sincere desire to build a sustainable business with strong ethics and beliefs.

Key words

compassionate, practical, balanced, common sense, adaptable, open, community, relationships, people, heart-felt, family, empathetic, harmony, corporate social responsibility, sustainability, environment, society, ethical, beliefs, considerate, protect, respect, enjoy, sympathetic, generous, helpful, humanitarian, philanthropic, attentive, thoughtful.

Jamie Oliver

The Chef Jamie Oliver was in tears following the reaction of *Dinner Ladies* at a school in the US: 'They don't understand me because they don't know why I'm here.' The caring chef was in the

(Contd)

CASE STUDY

West Virginia town of Huntington to address the obesity epidemic that accounts for two out of every three people in the US being overweight. The emotional moment appeared in the first episode of Jamie Oliver's 'Food Revolution' campaign. Oliver has placed a declaration on his website: 'I believe that every child in America has the right to fresh, nutritious school meals, and that every family deserves real, honest, wholesome food.' Oliver is appealing to the American nation to provide a better future for their children through nutrition. To back up his manifesto he has opened a walk-in advice centre called 'Jamie's Kitchen' on Huntington's Third Avenue.

Jamie Oliver first came to the public's attention in 1999 with his TV series *The Naked Chef* and the accompanying book. His energy and enthusiasm seemed endless. In 2000 he started appearing in Sainsbury's supermarket commercials and in 2002 he launched the Fifteen Foundation. The foundation gave 15 young people, from disadvantaged backgrounds, the opportunity of a career in the restaurant business. In 2005 he campaigned against the use of processed foods in school kitchens with the TV series *Jamie's School Dinners*. With his focus firmly kept on caring for the nation's diet, he followed with *Jamie's Ministry of Food*.

Oliver has extended his brand with the lifestyle magazine *Jamie*, a range of cookware called 'Jamie at home' and a chain of restaurants called 'Jamie's Italian'.

The Fifteen Foundation has been renamed as the Jamie Oliver Foundation. It was set up to train young people from deprived backgrounds to be chefs. Some of these youngsters had drifted into crime or dealt drugs. Oliver has taken on more than 120 hopefuls. The foundation's accounts show that 54 per cent of those trained have persevered and have jobs. The Fifteen London restaurant was followed by similar projects in Amsterdam, Cornwall and Melbourne.

The success of 'Jamie's School Dinners' campaign has improved not just the health of school children but their exam results, with a rise of 4.5 per cent in English SAT's results.

His enthusiasm for life is contagious and he is always creating – whether it is a new recipe, restaurant or trying to help people. He is extremely constructive, using his talent to help others, offering jobs to unemployed youths and helping to change people's perceptions about food. He has the confidence and courage to make a change for the good of all. You can tell that he really wants to help people.

He ranks at number 22 on the '2010 Giving List of Charitable Donors' published by *The Sunday Times* 'Rich List'. The chart calculates that Oliver's donations as a percentage of his wealth exceed those of Lord Rothschild.

The Jamie Oliver brand is focused on caring. Like Dame Anita Roddick, The Body Shop founder, Jamie Oliver is a passionate campaigner. He cares deeply about people and food and is often referred to in the media as 'The Kitchen Crusader'.

Communicative

Marshall McLuhan was a pioneer of modern media studies. He was a Canadian academic who analysed the impact of communication technology on society. He introduced the concept of 'The Global Village' to describe the effect of communication media by creating a shared state of mind through the instant transfer of information around the world. His book, *The Gutenberg Galaxy: The Making of Typographic Man* published in 1962, has been described as a prediction of the internet thirty years later. He introduced the idea of 'surfing' to describe how we skip from one piece of information to another and used the word 'mosaic' to describe a non-linear approach to accessing information. Mosaic is also the name of the first internet browser to open the world wide web (www) to the general public. The Mosaic browser used an intuitive interface that made it easier to surf the web. Mosaic evolved into Netscape, a pioneering brand of this new medium of communication. Its logo featured a capital 'N' straddling the globe ushering in a symbolic dawn. Netscape maintains 'the web is for everyone'.

The success of the web grew exponentially and it became the principal communication medium for commerce. Every brand has its website. Today the internet is a bewildering mass of information resembling McLuhan's idea of 'The Gutenberg Galaxy'.

The communication and culture magazine *Wired* honoured McLuhan's memory when they adopted him as their patron saint. The famous quote by Andy Warhol was influenced by McLuhan's thinking: 'In the future everyone will be famous for 15 minutes.'

A communicative brand facilitates the exchange of information. It improves life by enabling the exchange of ideas and brings people together.

Key words

informative, communication, friendly, informal, ideas, frank, simplicity, relevant, straightforward, honest, truthful, integrity, open, clear, authentic, expansive, trustworthy, entertaining, sociable, candid, enlightening, outgoing, talkative, conversable, focused, relationship.

CASE STUDY

Google

Google's self-proclaimed mission is to organize the world's information and make it universally accessible and useful. Larry Page and Sergey Brin founded the internet search engine in 1998 in the USA. It's the world's most popular search engine and the most visited website. Google is a free-to-use service that makes money from advertising.

Their success at organizing the world's information has led to most Web Masters having a preoccupation for a high Google ranking. Google offers tools to website owners for analysing their web traffic called Google Analytics. It has created a sub-industry of consultants promising you success and riches with a number one Google slot.

Google was not the first search engine, but it distinguished itself by being the easiest to use. This belies the fact that it uses highly sophisticated software. The search interface is now available in more than 110 languages.

Larry Page was a student at Stanford when he woke up from a dream with a vision for search. 'I was thinking: What if we download the whole web and just keep the links (*Googled: The End Of The World As We Know It*, Ken Auletta). His dream turned into 'PageRank' a process that evaluated a web page's worth by the quality of the links to and from it. Page shared his dream with his friend and fellow Stanford student Sergey Brin. They produced a prototype called 'BackRub', but in 1997 renamed it as the brand we are all now familiar with. Google is a word play on googol, the mathematical term for a number beginning with 1 followed by 100 zeros. Google represents infinite amount of information.

The Google brand is about simplicity and ease of use. It has become so successful and widely used that in June 2006 *The Oxford English Dictionary* added 'Google' as a verb.

If you are planning a journey, or considering moving house, Google Maps can prove to be an invaluable resource. The service began with a choice of traditional map or an aerial satellite view. But now site users can take a virtual walk with Google Street View. The service became available in the UK from May 2009. It had taken a year to photograph the 25 featured cities. The images are created using specially adapted cars with roof-mounted cameras. The images are then stitched together to create a virtual experience.

The brand has come under some criticism for this service with accusations of privacy infringement. In the Buckinghamshire village of Broughton, residents obstructed a Google camera van.

(Contd)

The European Union's privacy regulators have said that failure to give adequate notice could lead to legal action. Google's often quoted principle of 'Do no evil' has been questioned.

The perfect search engine ...would understand exactly what you mean and give back exactly what you want.

Larry Page, Google co-founder

Google staff are called Googlers and they enjoy a relaxed working atmosphere. On their website Google describe their culture as a small-company feel. 'Everyone eats in the office café, sitting at whatever table has an opening and enjoying conversations with Googlers from different teams'. Their commitment to innovation depends on everyone being comfortable with sharing ideas and opinions.

In 2006 Google added YouTube to its portfolio. It bought the video-sharing site for $1.65billion. YouTube allows users to upload and share their own videos. It's having an impact on how we view television and TV manufacturers are now including models with internet access and YouTube as a pre-set channel.

YouTube has proven to be an interesting communication medium with some surprising uses. The American Rock band Journey, famous for the hit 'Don't Stop Believin' recruited their new singer after seeing him on YouTube. Journey's guitarist Neil Schon was so impressed with the Philippine singer Arnel Pineda that he contacted him via email. After initial disbelief, Pineda flew to the States for a successful audition.

It has been a passion at the heart of Google to digitize the entire global library of books and make them available for search. They have encountered copyright problems but also a lot of cooperation from museums and publishers. This vision is another realization of 'The Gutenberg Galaxy'.

Knowledgeable

The knowledgeable brand earns its customers' trust and respect by sharing its expertise. There are some types of retailer that have an appalling reputation for ignoring their customers, giving incorrect information or simply being rude. This lack of service was illustrated in the 1980s sketch show *Not The Nine o'clock News*. The sketch, titled 'Gramophone', featured an awkward Mel Smith entering a hi-fi store to enquire about a gramophone player. The shop assistants, played by Rowan Atkinson and Griff Rhys Jones, mock and ridicule Smith about his ignorance of latest hi-fi equipment. This is only funny because it is so true of many music stores at the time. If you treat people poorly you cannot expect them to return! This is not how brands are built.

Knowledge is power.

Sir Francis Bacon, philosopher

The Black Cab and the London taxi driver are cultural icons. Black Cab drivers are famous for their chipper demeanour and encyclopaedic knowledge of the streets of London. They have to take a three-year training course called 'the knowledge' to gain deep understanding of London's streets. They learn an area covering a six-mile radius around Charing Cross. It takes perseverance to complete the training and three-quarters of applicants drop out. There are significant financial benefits from completing the course, as fares are typically higher than ordinary cabs.

The Black Cab is a trusted brand. The long training and proven knowledge distinguishes the cabbies from minicab drivers. To gain a licence, drivers have to be of 'good character' and there are strict rules regarding criminal convictions. They can charge more because they are trusted and have a reputation to uphold.

CASE STUDY

John Lewis

A department store where you are unlikely to get treated poorly is John Lewis. The chain of shops is unusual in that it is a partnership owned and run by its employees.

They have had the same slogan, 'Never Knowingly Undersold' for over 70 years. Mary Portas, the television presenter and retail adviser, thinks that their slogan still holds power. 'They are saying: "If you find someone selling a product cheaper, it's not because we've tried to put one over on you, it's just that we didn't know."' (*The Daily Telegraph*, 10 March 2010). This is a matter of trust and good, old-fashioned Englishness. The customers shop there, not for a bargain, but because John Lewis culturally understands what it is to be middle-class in England today.

Charlie Mayfield, John Lewis' executive chairman says that the key to John Lewis is trust. It's 'a faith built up over time, after the partnership's heavy emphasis on customer relations, underpinned by its "never knowingly undersold" promise'. These values are at the core of the business: 'The partnership has always been good at thinking about people, that's why it's so good at customer service – people make that happen' (*The Sunday Times*, 20 September 2009).

John Lewis scored highest with 91 per cent in the recent *Which?* 'Customer Satisfaction Index', which was conducted by the Institute of Customer Service. When the *Daily Mail* asked 'So which is Britain's best loved store?', John Lewis won hands-down.

Staff don't just own a share of the business, they take part in decisions and receive annual profit linked bonuses – which may explain why so many are helpful, and, best of all, well-informed.

The store offers free 'personal shoppers' to help you decide what to buy in the fashion and nursery departments.

In the 2010 BBC television programme *Inside John Lewis* Managing Director, Andy Street said 'the role of the business will be to edit choice and to provide a recommendation for a customer as to what really suits them.'

The John Lewis website says: 'We want to provide the best possible choice, value and service to customers. To be able to do this consistently, we need to know what customers want, which means constantly finding opportunities to listen to them, being open to feedback, and acting quickly on what they tell us, particularly if we've got something wrong. Many of our Partners have worked for the business for many years. They're interested in what they sell, and have excellent product knowledge'.

Inspirational

Napoleon Hill was a founding father of the self-help genre of literature. He wrote the highly successful book for self-development *Think and Grow Rich*. The focus of his books was to inspire people to achieve fulfilment.

> **What the mind of man can conceive and believe, it can achieve.**
>
> Napoleon Hill

Hill came from a modest background in the Appalachian Mountains of Virginia. His mother died when he was young and his stepmother encouraged his literacy. From the age of 15 he was contributing articles to local newspapers and later worked for Orison Swett Marsden's Magazine *Success*. The pivotal moment in his life came in 1908 when he interviewed the philanthropist and multi-millionaire businessman Andrew Carnegie. Carnegie believed in a simple process for personal success. Carnegie commissioned Hill to write a book that would make the philosophy of success accessible to the general public. In a period of twenty years he interviewed 500 of the most inspiring people of the age. Carnegie gave him personal introductions to the great and good, including Thomas Eddison, F.W. Woolworth and Henry Ford. The results of his work became the eight-volume *Law of Success* (1928).

Hill invited his readers to declare 'what you want from life – your idea of success. The only limit is you or the people you allow to stop you' and 'what will you give in return'.

The continued sales of his books are testament to his inspiration to people. His work was based on the insights he gained from inventors, industrialists, politicians and the great successes of the twentieth century. His focus on inspiration in over twenty years of interviews delivered a philosophy of success.

What is an inspirational brand? It is an honourable business model that is humble, noble, dignified and has a purpose. It will make sacrifices to fulfil its high ideals. These are inspirational businesses with very high standards, working for the common good. These businesses are sensitive, intuitive and have new ideas.

The Quaker movement in the UK created a number of household brand success stories that were inspired by social reform. The chocolate brands Cadbury, Fry's, Rowntree's and Terry's were all founded by Quakers. The boom in chocolate was driven by a desire to offer an alternative to alcohol.

Other brands with Quaker origins include Barclays and Lloyds banks, Clarks shoes, Bryant & May matches and Huntley & Palmers biscuits.

honourable, humble, noble, dignified, purpose, sacrifice, high ideals, standards, common good, sensitive, intuitive, ideas, decisive, authentic, enlightening, advancing, beneficial, constructive, enriching, expanding, helpful, influential, uplifting, awakening, meaningful, encouraging.

Oprah Winfrey

Oprah Winfrey is one of America's most powerful women. *The Oprah Winfrey Show* is the perfect vehicle for her warm personality and interests. It allows her to interact with the audience and involve them with her guests. She brings uplifting, inspirational and topical themes to her show. Before the term 'reality television' was used, Oprah was already sharing her real life diet and weight struggle with her audience. Oprah made television out of the daily issues that affected her viewers including relationships, health, education, faith and financial matters.

The Oprah Winfrey Show mission statement is: 'to use television to transform people's lives; to uplift, entertain and enlighten; to make viewers see themselves differently; and to bring a sense of fulfilment to every home'.

Oprah Winfrey's own life story is an inspiration. She was born into poverty in Mississippi and experienced great hardship in her early years. She was a gifted student and gained a full scholarship to Tennessee State University. At 17 she won a beauty pageant that led to a job with a local black radio station. She became the first black female news anchor at Nashville's WLAC-TV. In 1984 she moved to Chicago and began hosting WLS-TV's *AM Chicago*. Its success exceeded expectations and in ratings it overtook TV rival *Donahue*. In less than a year it was renamed *The Oprah*

(Contd)

CASE STUDY

Winfrey Show and has since become the highest rated talk show in television history.

In 1985, Oprah received nominations for both an Academy Award and a Golden Globe award for her acting debut. She played the part of 'Sofia' in *The Color Purple*, a film directed by Steven Spielberg.

Oprah is an international brand and her show is televised around the world to over 100 countries. Everything she touches seems to turn to gold. Experts that have appeared regularly on her shows have gone on to host their own successful programmes including Dr Phil and Dr Oz.

She is the arbiter of taste who decides what appears on her shows or is featured in her media operation. This creates consistency across the Oprah brand Harpo. Every aspect of the brand builds its reputation. Oprah is true to her outspoken ideals and returns a lot of her wealth to charitable causes.

The talk show formula has been credited with giving high-profile access to minority groups, softening attitudes through awareness. She has a great ability to empathize, share emotion and educate people. Her signature phrase is the 'Aha moment' used to describe the point when you gain an insight or wisdom that can change your life.

Oprah's Book Club has great power in turning new and sometimes obscure books into bestsellers. The format invites viewers and guests to read a novel and share their thoughts. It was emulated in Britain by the television hosts Richard and Judy with similar success.

Oprah runs her own media empire under the Harpo name (Oprah backwards!), which includes:

▶ *Harpo Inc.*
▶ *Harpo Films*
▶ *Harpo Radio*
▶ *Harpo Studios*

- *The Oprah Winfrey Show*
- *Oprah Winfrey Operating Foundations*
- *TV Development*
- *Oprah Store*
- *Oprah Winfrey Network (OWN).*

In 2004 Oprah was the first African-American philanthropist to feature on the *Business Week* Top 50 list.

In an interview with the magazine she described how her foundation exists to empower women, children, and families in communities with little opportunity. The foundation gives access to education and welfare. It provides scholarships to students who are committed to using their new skills to help their own neighbourhoods. The foundation builds schools and provides equipment to help educate children in need around the world.

Oprah has described how making other people happy is what gives her the greatest joy: 'I have a blessed life, and I have always shared my life's gifts with others ... I believe that to whom much is given, much is expected.' She uses her media empire as a catalyst to inspire and encourage people to make a difference for good.

Education is freedom. It provides the tools to affect one's own destiny.

Oprah Winfrey (*Business Week*, 29 November 2004)

In 1991 she testified before the US Senate Judiciary Committee to establish a national database of convicted child abusers. On 20 December 1993, President Clinton signed the National Child Protection Act or 'Oprah Bill' into law.

Oprah Winfrey's charitable work is carried out through three groups:

- *The Oprah Winfrey Foundation offers educational opportunities for children and families globally.*

(Contd)

- *The Oprah Winfrey Leadership Academy Foundation is a leadership academy for girls in South Africa.*
- *Oprah's Angel Network is a public charity that inspires people to make a difference in the lives of others. It gave $16.5 million to disaster recovery programmes following Hurricanes Katrina and Rita and the 2004 South Asian tsunami.*

Oprah Winfrey's positive mental attitude and her quest for self-improvement, has parallels with the life of Napoleon Hill. Both triumphed over disadvantaged backgrounds and continue to inspire people to success by helping them to help themselves.

TEST YOURSELF

▶ *What alternative name did Virgin consider?*

▶ *Apart from Hoover, what other brand names have become a generic?*

▶ *Who started his brand with a replacement for the wheelbarrow?*

▶ *Which global brand began life as 'BackRub'?*

▶ *Which high street brand is owned by its employees?*

▶ *Who changed the law and had a bill named after their personal brand?*

Part two
Brand creation

6

....

Brand culture

In this chapter you will learn about:
- *the importance of history in brand identity*
- *brand ethos*
- *the associations of language with brand*
- *the human face of brand*
- *brand leadership*
- *brand traditions*
- *brand-building using all five senses*
- *physical manifestations of brand*

Every organization develops its own culture, beginning with its
foundation, choice of name, first employees, business premises etc.
It grows organically, learning like a child, growing in confidence
until it matures into a sophisticated entity. This journey of
discovery is a valuable asset to the brand. It is often overlooked,
but the brand culture can be harnessed to great effect in building
the brand's status. Some of the world's largest brands understand
their cultural assets and use them to their full potential: Nike has
NikeTown; Lego has Legoland; Mercedes-Benz has Mercedes-Benz
World. These examples have created controlled environments
where every aspect is a realization of the brand. Visiting these
centres is like going to another country.

We are all inquisitive by nature and like to ask questions – Where
do you come from? How did it all start? Every brand, new or
old, has an opportunity to tell a story that supports the brand
promise. For example, if you are choosing a bottle of wine, you
will probably pick up the bottle and read the label first. On that

label will be a condensed cultural message – the age of the vintage, the location of the vineyard, the type of grape, the vintner's history, a description of the flavour and a suggestion of what food you can enjoy the wine with. This information – together with the shape of the bottle, the style of the label, screw top or cork – combine to communicate the brand's culture. The same is true of any product or service. Without first-hand experience we want to be sure of a brand's authenticity.

The big brand successes are like nations, rich in their own culture. They have a foundation story, ideology, special words, community, charismatic leaders' behavioural quirks and unique sensations.

Brand culture is:

- **History:** *The founder's story and origins of the brand.*
- **Ethos:** *The ideology and values of the brand.*
- **Language:** *The generation of special words and phrases to describe products and services unique to the brand.*
- **People:** *The community of employees, suppliers and customers.*
- **Leadership:** *The brand's champions.*
- **Traditions:** *Unique behaviour connected with the brand.*
- **Sensations:** *Look, hear, feel, smell, taste and intuition.*
- **Physical:** *Buildings, environment and objects.*

Let's take a closer look at how these cultural elements help to build a brand.

History

The brand story is the history of how it all began. If you've got a good story, people will listen to you – it's all part of buying into a brand. We connect with history through stories that recall past events and experiences. A great story makes a personal connection when we identify with it.

Legends are built and sometimes myths are made, but the essence of a good story has a ring of truth about it. Stories are good at grabbing our attention and conveying ideas and important messages. They help to focus the mind.

Storylines can be focused on certain brand attributes or they can celebrate people closely associated with the brand. It could be a story about leadership or exceptional performance and outstanding service. Brand stories should be inclusive, reflecting everyone's interests and capture the essence of the brand and what it stands for.

In pre-literate society, stories were used to pass knowledge through the generations. Storytelling is still a part of how we share history. The brand story is like a campfire story – if it's good we will be gripped and relay it to our friends. Great stories stay with you.

A good brand story should:

▶ *be simple*
▶ *be credible*
▶ *be emotional*
▶ *be surprising*
▶ *support the brand.*

Aston Martin

The origins of the name and its badge tell a great story of sporting prowess. The British luxury car brand began life in 1913 when Lionel Martin and Robert Bamford joined forces to sell Singer cars. In 1914 they achieved success at the Aston Clinton Hill Climb in Buckinghamshire. The badge that we recognize today was designed in 1932 by the famous racing driver and journalist S.C.H. 'Sammy' Davis. He had a keen interest in Egyptology and was inspired by the open-winged flight of the scarab beetle. The scarab is a symbol of transformation or renewal of life.

(Contd)

Davis was a leading writer with *Autocar* magazine and a member of the famous Bentley Boys, driving 'Old number 7' in the winning team at the 1927 Le Mans 24-hour race. How he won that race is another brand-building story of valour and courage.

Think of all the urban myths and how fast they get shared. A great story can be viral, spreading quickly by word of mouth or through the web. A good story that aligns with your brand values can strengthen the emotional connection between your customers and your brand.

Ethos

The brand ethos is the guiding beliefs that define an organization's view on the world and how it can contribute to making it a better place to live. The brand's ethos has no value if the organization is not actively involved in pursuing its ideal. For example, a brand that promotes an image of youthful vitality but uses child labour is a confused message. The ethos of the brand must relate to its purpose.

The brand ethos must be a genuinely held set of beliefs. Dame Anita Roddick founded The Body Shop chain on a heart-felt concern for ethical consumerism. She championed Fair Trade, environmental and social issues and placed them at the heart of her business brand. An ethos should be actively pursued and not just used as a convenient social responsibility tagline for marketing purposes. A strong ethos should connect everyone in the organization in a common goal and needs to be straightforward and achievable to be embraced by the whole team.

'Corporate social responsibility' (CSR) is the obligatory policy for every large organization, but it too must be heart-felt to be credible. It was common in the Victorian era for industrialists to exercise philanthropy with their newfound wealth. Andrew Carnegie built his wealth on iron but carefully gave back to society with the gift of libraries, universities and museums. These charitable actions were linked to the founding beliefs of the companies' founders and were an integral part of what they stood for. Today there is a tendency for CSR to be bolted on and used in public relations to create goodwill and respectability.

The clothing brand Benetton was one of the first to promote social issues through its advertising, and deliberately used provocative images to stimulate debate. The series of advertisements did not include their clothes and worked on raising awareness of issues that concerned the brand's organization, for example, AIDS, multiculturalism and faith. In doing so they could connect with and attract the attention of the wider community.

The Co-operative

The Co-operative can trace its history back to 1844 when the Rochdale Pioneers Society was established as a consumer co-operative. It shared a dividend of its profits with its customers, which is now popularly known as the 'divi'. Since the Co-operative's beginnings it has championed a sound ethical stance. In 1985 they ruled that no 'own-brand' toiletries and household products could be tested on animals. Together with the Royal Society for the Prevention of Cruelty to Animals (RSPCA) they co-sponsored a private members' bill to require better labelling of products tested on animals. In 1992 the Co-operative Bank became the world's first bank to introduce a customer-led ethical policy. This gave thousands of people the opportunity to choose a bank that does not do business with unethical companies and organizations. In 1997 they launched the first biodegradable credit card – backed by Green Peace. In 1998 it began stocking Fairtrade products, guaranteeing a better deal for developing nations. In 1999 they launched Smile – the UK's first full internet bank, and two years later they introduced braille to their 'own-brand' medicine packaging. In 2006 the international institute AccountAbility proclaimed the Co-operative officially the UK's most trusted retailer.

(Contd)

CASE STUDY

The Co-operative has grown in strength, placing its ethos at the heart of everything it does. Membership is open to all that share their values and principles:

Co-operative values:
self-help, self-responsibility, democracy, equality, equity, solidarity.

Co-operative ethical values:
openness, honesty, social responsibility, caring for others.

Co-operative principles:
voluntary and open membership, democratic member control, member economic participation, autonomy and independence, education, training and information, co-operation amongst co-operatives, concern for community.

A strong ethos can be a competitive advantage against businesses with no obvious ethical stance; it also makes it harder to emulate. Consumers that share the brand's ethos are more likely to develop an ongoing relationship when the brand helps them express what they believe. Strongly held principles go hand in hand with integrity, and consumers are more likely to trust a brand that maintains a consistent stance.

Language

If you listen to a radio programme, you can build a picture of what the presenter is like based on their tone of voice and use of language. By listening to their voice it is possible to judge their age, education, social status or even their nationality or the region they come from. Our choice of words can link us to a particular part of the country. A dialect will have its own special words and phrases that present a unique verbal identity: Geordie, Cockney and West Country among many.

Brands have dialects too. If you have ever asked for a 'Frappuccino', then you have been conversing in a brand dialect. The same word might draw a blank at any coffee shop other than Starbucks.

The choice of product names and the language used to describe them can be a potent asset for building the brand but it is often ignored. What is the brand actually saying and is it inviting you to take part? Language is a sophisticated way of promoting your brand and can become endemic. Phrases including McDonald's 'I'm lovin' it' enjoy popular use after repetitive exposure through advertising. The choice of words can alienate or attract; they can help the brand position itself by connecting with a particular niche group. 'Never knowingly undersold', is a promise that connects directly with middle-class values, with its sense of fair play and respectability. This phrase works for John Lewis because it is natural for the retail group and expresses its personality. The brand has an accent that must be consistently applied. Imagine if a Geordie friend of yours began using Cockney rhyming slang – the impact would be either bewildering or very funny. The same rules apply to a brand – we get used to the voice.

Bic Biro

Like Hoover, Band-Aid and Thermos, Biro is a generic word in widespread use to describe a category of product – the ballpoint pen. László József Bíró was the inventor of the modern ball pen and presented his first design at the Budapest National Fair in 1931 and seven years later patented the design in Paris. He moved to Argentina to escape the Nazis and formed Biro Pens of Argentina. The Royal Air Force adopted the pen as it did not leak and remained functional at high altitude. The British government bought the licensing rights to the pen's patent for the war effort. In 1950 Marcel Bich bought the patent from Biro that led to the ubiquitous Bic Biro. How many words have been written with a biro since?

Language can be used to keep a brand in a niche and cliques enjoy using a secret language to keep unwanted outsiders out. This is best illustrated by technology, when specialists baffle novices with phrases and words that only someone 'in the know' can understand. This raises the bar to the entry level of a brand and can raise its prestige if managed carefully.

People

Have you ever walked into a shop and felt uncomfortable? Perhaps you have been ignored or, worse still, pounced upon. The employees are the human face of the brand and act as its ambassadors. They are given a huge responsibility with the brand's image. There is a great opportunity for the retail sector to capitalize on this interaction and turn it into a positive experience. Even when staff do not have direct contact with customers their attitude and behaviour can affect how the brand is perceived. White Van Man has become a cliché for inconsiderate driving, but behind the wheel of every van is a business ambassador. The van is a commercial vehicle and bad road use is bad for commerce, especially if the company name is painted on the side.

Do successful brands employ a certain type of person? Can a recruitment policy create a community of like-minded people? To join the British Army you must be at least 148cm tall and to be a Black Cab driver you must pass 'the knowledge'. All organizations have entry requirements to help them select the right type of person – but clones do not build brands. People bring the brands they work for to life and a shared enthusiasm and belief in their brand is contagious in attracting new staff and customers. Some organizations get their culture so right that they don't have to advertise for staff and there are waiting lists of people queuing for the opportunity to join.

Butlins Red Coats

The first Butlins Holiday Camp opened in Skegness in 1936 with a capacity for 1,000 guests. Sir Billy Butlin formed the company on the basis of offering a week's holiday for a standard week's wage, and the brand continues to offer value today. The brand now has three sites including Minehead, Bognor Regis as well as Skegness and entertains 1.5 million guests a year. Butlin had spent some of his childhood in Canada and took inspiration from the Canadian Mounties' uniform for the famous Red Coats' blazers. Butlins employs over 3,000 people, over 100 of which are Red Coats.

The Red Coats are the face and personality of the brand. Their uniform remained largely unchanged until the fashion designer Zandra Rhodes created a new version in the 1980s and it has been redesigned several times since. The Red Coats are holiday hosts who perform on stage and look after children's and sporting activities. Over 3,000 candidates applied to become a Red Coat in 1998 and queues formed at London's Hippodrome for auditions. In 1999 the brand launched the Red Coat Academies of Excellence to teach skills ranging from stage management to the performance of musical theatre.

Each year there are thousands of applicants to join and current candidates are invited to upload a video online with YouTube to help their audition. A strong emphasis is placed on the ability to get along with people and take a team-playing role. A natural cheerful disposition is required at all times.

In January 2010 Butlins were the first company to win the Customer Service Employer of the Year Award. Allan Lambert, Head of Retail Sales Bourne Leisure (owner of Butlins) said: 'We will continue to invest time, money and resources in our guests and team members, to maintain the highest levels of sales and service superiority into the New Year and for years to come.' The Butlins brand clearly values its people and helps develop their potential.

(Contd)

The opportunity to be a Red Coat is valued as a great start in show business and there is an impressive roll call of talented names who started their careers at Butlins: Francis Rossi (Status Quo), Ian Watkins (H from Steps), Johnny Ball (*Think of a Number* and *Playschool*), Des O'Connor, Jimmy Tarbuck, and Ringo Starr who was working in a resort band when he got the call to join the Beatles!

The recruitment of staff is an opportunity to select people who will represent the brand and will promote it effectively. The Human Resources department, or those responsible for staff recruitment, have a guiding role in the sustainability of the brand. Every employee should be able to answer basic questions about their company – what it does, its products and services, who owns it, how long it has been running etc. An interest in the business you work for reveals a pride and an active part in the brand's welfare.

Every employee should understand their role in the organization and their part in building the brand's image. A spirit of common purpose, loyalty and community will convey an attractive brand image. If employers take care to develop their staff and reward them for their performance, it can have significant returns in brand-building and community morale.

Leadership

Great brands need strong leaders who guide and inspire their staff and customers. They convince us and stimulate the surrounding community. They reach out and transform. When a brand is in the news for the wrong reasons, it is the leadership that will be scrutinized. These testing times can make or break a brand. When a brand is involved in a dispute the leadership will be required to speak with the media to allay customers' concerns. They may be called to make difficult decisions to protect the brand from long-term damage. Like a nation, a brand needs its leaders to be decisive and bold – it's not a job for a shrinking violet. Some brand leaders are so closely associated with their brand that they become the manifestation of the brand. It's the same with nations – iconic leaders can come to encapsulate the national mood, for example, Mahatma Gandhi, Nelson Mandela and Winston Churchill.

It takes all kinds of people – have you got what it takes to be a great brand leader? These are some of the common characteristics:

Passion
▶ *They are driven by passion and love what they do.*
▶ *They evangelize passionately about the brand they believe in.*
▶ *They surround themselves with people who support that vision.*
▶ *They communicate their enthusiasm and empathize with their customers.*
▶ *They see the bigger picture and don't get lost in the detail.*
▶ *They motivate their staff and customers.*

Difference
▶ *They don't just do things well, they do them better.*
▶ *They are not afraid to be first, to shake up the status quo and break out of the mould.*
▶ *They surpass our expectations.*
▶ *They have dreams and aspirations.*

Customers
▶ *They make it their business to ensure a great customer experience.*
▶ *They empathize with the customer and staff.*
▶ *They value customer feedback and address negative responses.*
▶ *They are aware of how the brand is perceived.*
▶ *They encourage customer and staff interaction.*

Communication
▶ *They tell a great story about the brand.*
▶ *They engage the media and manage the way the brand is perceived.*
▶ *They are well read and gain inspiration from fellow leaders.*

- ▶ *They convince and share their view with their customers and staff.*
- ▶ *They attract and retain good people by rewarding them.*
- ▶ *They foster a community spirit and are caring.*

Happiness
- ▶ *They promote a happy working environment.*
- ▶ *They make fun part of the working culture.*
- ▶ *They make work a rewarding experience and staff take home happy memories.*

Determination
- ▶ *They can think on their feet and cope with the unexpected*
- ▶ *They take risks.*
- ▶ *They are proud of their organization.*

Good leadership is fundamental to the success of a brand. It is the role of the business leader to champion the brand, conveying their passion and enthusiasm to everyone.

Traditions

Every nation has its own unique customs and traditions, from seasonal events to celebrated anniversaries, for example: Guy Fawkes Night (Bonfire Night) in the UK and Bastille Day in France. Brands create traditions too and have the power to affect our behaviour and influence our actions. Some notable brands have combined national traditions with their own identity to embed themselves in our consciousness. The New Zealand National Rugby Union Team is more commonly known as the All Blacks. They are closely associated with the Haka dance, in particular the 'Ka mate, Ka mate' which they perform before matches. The complex dance is an expression of passion, vigour and identity and is derived from the indigenous Maori population of New Zealand. It carries high social importance in the welcoming of visitors and the ability to perform it well is critical. The All Blacks are a great rugby brand and their Haka is a unique tradition linked to their identity.

Another famous brand that has combined cultural tradition with its brand identity is Coca-Cola.

Coca-Cola and Christmas

If you think of Father Christmas (Santa Claus) it is easy to visualize a large jolly chap with a long white beard dressed in red robes, but this wasn't always the fixed image of the generous patron of the Yuletide season. In Charles Dickens' *A Christmas Carol* the ghost of Christmas Present reveals an older description of his image, dressed in a fur-lined green robe and wearing a wreath of holly on his head. There are a host of figures who have been said to have inspired his legend, gathered from the world's cultures, including St Nicholas and Odin. He had previously been visualized in different shapes and forms – but Coca-Cola take responsibility for fixing his image to the large happy fellow that we recognize today.

The Coca-Cola Company explain in their online history that they began using Santa Claus in their Christmas advertising in 1931. At this time they used magazine adverts depicting St Nicholas as a kind and jolly man in a red suit.

In 1930 the commercial artist Fred Mizen painted an advertising image of Santa in a crowded department store drinking a bottle of Coke. Coca-Cola were keen to position Coke as a drink for all seasons, and not just warm weather, in Depression Era America.

In 1931, The Coca-Cola Company commissioned the illustrator Haddon Sundblom to create images of a 'real' Santa Claus for advertising and not a father impersonating Santa Claus. Sundblom took inspiration from the poem "Twas the Night Before Christmas' by Clement Clark Moore. The poem described St Nicholas in the following words, 'He was chubby and plump, a right jolly old elf'.

(Contd)

His depiction based on this poem has become the *de facto* image of Santa and is used to this day.

Sundblom's images are highly collectable, prized pieces of commercial art and have even been exhibited at The Louvre in Paris. Today Coca-Cola's Santa is as ubiquitous as the drink itself.

Sensations

There are cities in this world that you could identify even if you were blindfolded. Our ability to see, hear, touch, smell and taste allows us to experience the world in multiples of sensations. Each sense combines together to deliver a unique experience. As we move through a building we can appreciate differences in acoustics, temperature or ambience. We know from people who have lost their sight that they are able to amplify other senses to build a mental picture of their environment. The delicate engagement of each sense creates an impression of our location that makes a unique experience. If you have travelled the world you will know how each capital city has such different characteristics. If you have been to Paris and I asked you to picture it you could probably describe the smells, music and sights that give it a unique identity.

Brands have a great opportunity to engage our senses and capitalize on sensory branding. Some already do it very well. Think of your favourite brand, or the brand you hope to create, and ask yourself: how does it fill your senses and could you still identify it, if you removed any element of sight, sound, touch, smell or taste?

Sight: If a picture is worth a thousand words then it's not surprising that we lean so heavily on the visual sense in branding. From colour to monochrome, from light to dark, shape, materials, finish, photography, illustration, typography and composition – all are combined together to create a unique design style that identifies the brand visually.

Sound: Acoustics are the soundscape of an environment. An echo can be a significant factor in the identification of your brand. We can detect the height of the ceiling or the distance of the walls from the way our voices travel in a room. A recent medical breakthrough has helped blind people to see by making a clicking sound with the tongue. The sound echoes off objects and by judging the time lapse in the echo they can estimate the nature of the object. It is even possible to determine the surface of the object by the tone and timbre of the echo. On a subconscious level we all detect differences in acoustics. They form part of the subconscious branding of an environment. Most retail chains use standard shop formats, and each venue shares the same furnishings and dimensions. This creates an acoustic soundscape unique to the location and forms part of the retail experience.

In more obvious ways sound is constantly used by brands whether deliberately or not. The whir of the laptop, the click of the keyboard as you type in information. It could be the choice of music played in a shopping mall or the music you are played when holding on the telephone. Consider the impact that you have in controlling sound and how it adds to the overall experience of the brand. Is it necessary to play Vivaldi's *Four Seasons* down the telephone or could a different choice be more meaningful to your customer? Really think about your choice of music, as I was once put on hold by a building management company who played 'Are you Lonesome Tonight?' by Elvis whilst I waited to be connected!

Touch: Texture and finish have an important role to play in evaluating quality. We are always touching things to see how they feel, from clothing to cars. In every field of consumerism we make decisions based on touch. You want to try them on, take it for a test run, and check if the fruit is ripe. So how do we recognize a brand through touch? It can be the choice of material. Physical products have surfaces and the choice of the materials is evidence of their quality and monetary value – as the saying goes, 'feel the quality'.

Smell: Apart from a perfume brand, you might not consider smell to be one of your priorities. But then think how you feel if you meet someone with a bad body odour – it can be off-putting; the same is true for brands – scent can be persuasive too! Hospitality brands, especially hotels will frequently use scent to create a pleasant ambience, but smell is open to all brands. New cars have a new car smell – so smell can be used to say 'new'. The scents of leather and wood can remind you that you are driving a luxury car, for example. Smell is a subtle tool that can have a subliminal effect on your brand. We use smell to detect if something is rotten or fresh, it's something we do all the time in a supermarket. You cannot avoid a scent – it's in the air we breathe.

Taste: It may seem like the hardest sense to make use of outside of the food and restaurant trade, but taste can be used to build a service brand too. Think of all the meetings that you have at work and how many cups of coffee and tea you have consumed. If the coffee is good, you feel welcome and valued. A bad cuppa literally leaves a bad taste in the mouth.

Intuition: Intuition is the gut feeling we get when everything feels just right. We may not admit to intuition, but it can influence our choices. We all know when something is wrong but just can't put our finger on it. You may try to manipulate the senses to work in favour for your brand but intuition is one you have no control over.

Physical

The buildings and monuments we create are an expression of our culture. A capital city is usually a collage of building styles representing different ages, ideals and status. Commerce is responsible for some of the most beautiful buildings on our city skylines. The Chrysler Building in New York is an art deco monument of the high day of the automobile. Walter Chrysler was the chairman of the Chrysler Corporation and the owner of the skyscraper. Many of the architectural details including the building's gargoyles are based on Chrysler automobile products, such as the detailing on the Plymouth car. At the time of its completion the Chrysler Building was the world's tallest building in 1930.

Some of the greatest architecture has been built by brands. The great age of steam witnessed a building spree that built stations in the form of cathedrals. These temples to travel were a proud declaration of the might of the companies that ran them. The Midland Railway opened St Pancras station in central London in 1868. It was the southern terminus of a line that ran from London to Yorkshire. The arched train shed was the largest single-span roof in the world. One of the most recognizable features of St Pancras station is the red-brick, Grade 1 listed, Gothic-front façade. This magnificent building is known as the Midland Great Hotel and was designed by Sir Gilbert Scott and completed in 1876.

Both the Chrysler Building and the Midland Great Hotel were grand statements and testament to the power of the organizations behind them – they communicated the message 'we are here to stay and you can trust our brand'.

The famous painting 'Rain, Steam and Speed – The Great Western Railway' was painted by the great artist J.M.W. Turner in 1844. It features a steam train passing over the Maidenhead Bridge and the objects are barely recognizable in the intensity of colour and use of light. The engineer Isambard Kingdom Brunel designed the bridge and also created his engineering triumph – The Great Western Railway (also known as 'God's Wonderful Railway'). This famous painting is an early example of art inspired by enterprise.

The arrival of Pop Art in the 1950s heralded a movement that was accessible to all by its appropriation of mass-media images. It drew heavily on advertising, packaging and the collateral of mass consumption. By re-using everyday objects a cross cultural language was created that helped us view everyday objects from a fresh perspective, for example, Andy Warhol's 'Campbell's

Soup Cans'. There is great art in the functionality of products and their packaging. A recent survey published in *The Daily Telegraph* newspaper listed Britain's top five most loved bottle designs: Heinz Tomato Ketchup, HP Sauce, Worcestershire Sauce, Colman's Mustard and Bovril. These distinctive bottle shapes are immediately recognizable on the supermarket shelves and differentiate their brands.

Today brands are still using architecture and buildings as grand statements of their brand. Mercedes-Benz World at Brooklands in Weybridge is a brand centre spread over three floors. It was opened in 2006 and hosts its own museum collection, a full range of current models, a restaurant and driving track. It is situated on the site of the historic Brooklands Circuit, the world's first purpose-built racetrack and the location of the first British Grand Prix. The style of the building with its central hub and three-pointed star are suggestive of the radiator grill of a Mercedes-Benz. It is a palace to the brand and, like Nike Town and Legoland, it reflects its brand values in the style of the building, interior and presentation.

TEST YOURSELF

▶ *What stories can you tell about your favourite brands?*

▶ *Which brand combines ethics with beauty?*

▶ *Can you explain the ethos behind a business for which you have worked?*

▶ *Where would you buy a 'frappuccino'?*

▶ *Name a brand with excellent customer service.*

▶ *Name a strong leader.*

▶ *Think of a tradition which could build your company brand.*

▶ *How could the senses help your company?*

7

Brand strategy

In this chapter you will learn about:
- *establishing a working group*
- *key branding criteria*
- *research*

The start of a new brand programme is comparable to an expedition of discovery. The expedition leader will need to brief their team on the objective of the exercise. They will explain what they are hoping to achieve and for whose benefit, where the operation will take place, the kit that will be used and the expected outcome. A lot of planning and research will have gone into preparing the operational brief, a reconnaissance will have been undertaken to survey the territory and an analysis will have been made of the team's strengths and weaknesses. The more that is known about the field of operation the greater the advantage of the task force. If you want a successful outcome for your expedition, then you will need to start with good information. The information is then analysed so that strategic recommendations can be made. These are presented in a brief to empower the task force to succeed in their mission. Just like our expedition analogy, branding is rewarding and can be very exciting.

A new brand programme may be commissioned for a variety of reasons:

- *new organization, product or service*
- *re-launch of an existing organization, product or service*

- *uniting a group*
- *creating a higher profile*
- *attracting and retaining staff*
- *new ownership*
- *attracting investors*
- *attracting customers.*

Establishing a working group

The first stage in creating a brand is to establish a working group which is divided into two parties:

- **The management team:** *Led by the organization's principal figure (owner, entrepreneur, Managing Director or Chief Executive) and assisted by key management figures.*
- **The brand team:** *Managed by a senior brand consultant and their team. They will need the experience and maturity to engage with senior management.*

We do not advise appointing an internal brand team. It is rare that people within an organization are able to interview their colleagues objectively without political interference. The brand team should be a neutral third party that is unconnected to the respective organization. Selecting the right partner is like choosing any other professional service. Evaluate their past work, find out what their clients think of them, check their reputation and fees and, above all, decide if these are people that you would like to work with. You may be spending rather a lot of time together!

The ideal brand consultant will be confident and at ease with senior management. They will be required to ask some direct and sensitive questions, but the process should be fun and engaging for all. At the end of the research the brand consultant will be required to analyse their findings and make strategic recommendations in a concise briefing document.

There are different kinds of brand consultancies. Some consultants' strengths lie in the forward planning and strategy, others excel at the creative execution, and a third group will offer both services. You will need to decide if you want the same team to work from strategy through creative execution and onto final implementation.

Key branding criteria

The brand working party will work together to answer the key branding criteria, which are:

- **Purpose:** *What does the brand do?*
- **Vision:** *What is the brand's ambition?*
- **Values:** *What does the brand stand for?*
- **Mission statement:** *How is the brand going to achieve its vision?*
- **Proposition:** *Why do I need the brand?*
- **Position:** *How does the brand compare with its competitors?*
- **Personality:** *What is the brand's character?*
- **Audience:** *Who is interested in the brand?*

CRITERIA IN DETAIL

Purpose
Every organization, product or service must have a reason for being. A brand's purpose is the benefit it provides and may be defined as the thing that it does to make the world a better place. For example: does a mechanic repair cars or keep you in motion? Are they in the repair trade or the mobility business? The brand's purpose should be clear and easy to understand and be a benefit that can be experienced straightaway. Making money is not a valid purpose because it is a necessity of any commercial enterprise.

Vision
A brand vision is an ambition for the future; it's where you want to be in five or ten years' time. It is a goal to be worked towards

and will deliver a clear benefit to all concerned. A great vision can inspire and consolidate a community in a common goal. It is both emotional and passionate. The vision should be measurable and have a clear conclusion.

A vision should be both motivational and inspiring and *not* be about making lots of money so that the founder can retire in luxury! It should be directed at the management, staff and shareholders.

Guidelines for a brand vision:

▶ *Focus on the destination and not the journey.*
▶ *Avoid words like: best, leading and first.*
▶ *Make it measurable – or how will you know when you have achieved it?*
▶ *Ensure management champion the vision.*
▶ *Don't make it too easy – it must be heroic and require effort.*
▶ *Make sure it is easily understood.*

Values

A brand's values are what it stands for and what it believes in; they are the guidelines that form its moral compass. Values provide direction on how to behave in any given situation; they dictate the behaviour of the brand and influence decisions. The values you choose can be applied to everything, including the product experience, choice of staff, and how you react in a crisis. Values should be very clear, authentic and resonate with everyone inside the organization. They should be clearly understood by employees, adopted by them and consistently acted on. The brand's values should help the organization achieve the vision and not restrict it. A brand should have no more than a handful of values if they are to be remembered and acted upon. These values can be ranked in order of importance. Strong brands are respected for their values and are defined by them.

When we are young we have values imposed upon us, the values of our family, our school, club or sport. As we grow older we adopt our own values, the principles we hold dear. We do not all share the same values and that's what makes us interesting. We can predict how our friends might behave in a situation by knowing their values, and so it is with a brand. In Chapter 5: Brand focus, we looked at the qualities that have defined some of the world's most interesting brands: Pioneering, Creativity, Innovation, Caring, Communication, Knowledge and Inspiration. Your brand can be defined by its values and stand for something!

Mission statement

A mission statement combines the brand's purpose, vision and values in a brief declaration directed at management, staff and shareholders. It is a strategic communication that is clearly worded and accessible to all. The mission statement will clarify: what we do; what the brand's ambition is; what the brand stands for. The mission statement should be no longer than this paragraph.

Proposition

The brand proposition is the unique selling point (USP) that differentiates it from its competitors. It is the compelling reason why you need it and should be no more than a single sentence.

For example: <u>Brand X</u> is the only _____ that _____ !

This is the big idea behind the brand and the promise of satisfaction. A great proposition should be memorable, build value, have relevance and resonate with the customer. It should stand the test of time and be credible. It's the reason why Volvo is about safety and Audi is about technology.

Positioning

In a crowded marketplace it is difficult to stand out if you are the seventh best-selling brand. Most marketplaces are overcrowded and cluttered and so in order to succeed, a brand must stand out and differentiate itself. The opportunity is to identify the attributes that differentiate your brand and promote your brand as the leader in that niche category. You promote the category as much as you promote your brand and consequently own the leading position in your customer's mind. The objective of the exercise is to simplify your customer's choice so that there is only one option – your brand.

For example: bladeless desk fan = Dyson.

Personality
The brand personality is the brand's distinctive character, including communication, behaviour and visual style. Every organization, product or service has a personality but the opportunity is to capitalize on it so that it becomes a valuable differentiator. A brand with a strong personality has a greater chance of encouraging a deeper relationship with the consumer.

Numatic

Europe's favourite, fast and friendly professional vacuum cleaner is manufactured by Numatic in the UK. It is a small, red vacuum cleaner with a bowler hat, a smiley face and a name – Henry! The family has been extended to include Hetty (pink), George (green), Charles (blue) and James (yellow). The product not only works well and is good value for money, but it has a strong personality. Numatic have taken a very functional mundane household product and used a friendly personality to create a strong brand.

Personality is the part of the brand that people get passionate about because it's emotional. The competitive advantage is that a personality is very hard to duplicate, for example the Virgin brand personality is an extension of its founder Richard Branson.

Audience
Who are your customers? Who are you working with? What organizations are supporting you? These are the groups of people that form the brand's audience. This audience is never passive; it is an interactive community of people with an interest in the enterprise. It is a helpful exercise to compile a list of all the various groups who interact with the brand. They may include some or all of the following:

> Customers | Prospects | Suppliers | Partners | Employees |
> Management | Resellers | Advisers | Associations | Government
> | Investors | Financiers | Media | Charities | Competitors

It is important to profile this wider audience before you take a brand to market. Depending on the type of organization, product or service certain groups of the audience will have a greater impact on the brand.

Consider the lifestyle habits of your main target market – what is important and relevant to them? For example, what car do they drive? What newspaper do they read? What level of education do they have and where do they live, shop, eat or holiday etc? The objective is to visualize a virtual world around the brand – built on its external influences. It can help to produce a map depicting these influences; the brand is placed in the centre of the map like the middle of a target and the brand influences radiate out with the strongest, closest to the centre.

Brand map example

A brand map for the external influences of a quality department store would place the brand in the centre of a target. A series of circles will radiate out from the centre to represent the value of each influence. Close to the circle's centre could be the words Middle Class and radiating out could be Aspirational, Further Education, Career, Professionalism, Prestige Car, Broadsheet Newspaper, Holidays in France, Classical Music, Outdoor pursuits etc. The words and associations create a picture of the external influences surrounding the brand.

Research

We recommend that the working group takes a tour of the organization's premises to share an insight into the everyday running of the business. The branding team may take a camera to record reference material. It is important to take an interest in the operation of the business, its products and services and get a general feel for the environment and culture.

Collect all existing marketing collateral for the brand and its competitors. If you have the resources it can help to create a video and include comments from the general public regarding your business sector, for example asking a person on the street for their thoughts on this type of company, product or service.

Research to consider:

▶ **Marketing collateral for the organization and its competitors:** *this could include: stationery, forms, publications, advertising, press releases, newspaper coverage, trade press coverage, packaging, sales literature, websites, blogs, twitter, social media exposure, exhibitions, uniform, badges, merchandise, etc.*
▶ **Internal information:** *for example history and structure of the company.*
▶ **Research reports:** *this could include trends, statistics and reports from industry, trade associations and local and central government.*

INTERVIEW QUESTIONS

The ideal length of time for an interview is one and a half hours. The mood should be kept friendly and informal and not feel like an interrogation or job interview. The interviewee must not have advance warning of the questions and a fast instinctive response is preferred. We have found that some interviewees misinterpret the question but still give very insightful answers. The point to emphasize is that there are no right or wrong answers; the exercise is to gather heartfelt opinions. The skill of the interviewer is to make the interviewee feel comfortable about talking and to gather information. The interviewer will not only be monitoring the answers but making observations on the ambience, mood and environment.

Like an Agatha Christie detective, the skilled interviewer will use their senses to gather a deeper insight into the organization. We all have the ability to pick up on details and nuances. Often these are absorbed subconsciously but they build an impression of people and their environment.

The interviewer will notice the interviewee's body language, personal presentation and their work space environment. A quick glance around someone's desk will often reveal family photos, a desk screensaver of their favourite destination or ideal car. These details are often very revealing and give you insight into the people behind the brand. The skilled interviewer will listen very carefully to the answers and notice where emphasis is placed and the style in which the questions are answered. For example, is the person expressive or reserved? Did the interviewee welcome you with a limp or firm handshake? Is the environment hygienic, tidy and fresh or stale and odorous? Does the host make the interviewer feel welcome with real coffee, etc? Is there any effort at hospitality? Are the drinks freshly made or are they instant, and how are they served – plastic cup or china cup and saucer? These observations can give a unique insight into the personality and priorities of the organization and its people. The interviewer should take note of their gut feelings – these will be especially strong after the first meeting. They should ask themselves: is this a happy environment?

Brand consultants need to be intuitive and sensitive in order to pick up important information which might otherwise be missed. In order to fully understand an organization, you need to understand the owner first – how do they behave, communicate and what is their personal style? This information will be helpful for creating the brand identity.

Creating a perfect brand is partly down to the ability to read a situation and interpret accurately. The brand consultant is like a gold prospector who carefully processes the raw material to find the golden nugget that will turn into a perfect brand.

THE QUESTIONS

Each group of questions is headed by a key question. You may use any or all of the questions. They are intended only for guidance.

Key question: What is your marketplace like?
- *What is the mood and attitude like?*
- *How big is this market?*
- *How old is this market?*
- *Is this a new type of market?*
- *What is the nature of your business?*
- *How will the product or service be sold?*
- *Have any reports revealed any interesting insights?*
- *Are there any public issues with this market area; either ethical or environmental?*
- *Is this market profitable?*
- *Is this market in a state of constant change?*
- *Does this market attract a particular type of person?*
- *Have there been any past incidents that have had an adverse effect?*
- *What is the perception from within the organization of this market?*
- *Do the financial and political communities have a view on this type of organization?*

Key question: What are your competitors like?
- *Are there any established main players in this market?*
- *Is there any significant competition?*
- *Do you admire any of your competitors?*
- *What do the main competitors stand for?*
- *What are your competitors' key strengths and weaknesses?*
- *What are your key strengths and weaknesses?*
- *Which demographic do they serve?*
- *How do they market themselves?*
- *Is there an available gap in positioning?*
- *How are you different from your competitors?*
- *What is their financial situation?*
- *Does a competitor monopolize the market?*

- *How many competitors are there in the market?*
- *Are the competitors significantly different?*
- *How do competitors structure their organization?*

Key question: Describe a typical customer?
- *Who are your customers?*
- *Why would a customer choose you instead of the market leader?*
- *Is any information available to describe a typical customer?*
- *Are they male or female and what is the percentage split?*
- *What age are they?*
- *What standard of education have they achieved?*
- *What income bracket do they belong to?*
- *What is their family situation, e.g. living alone, with children, etc?*
- *Where do they live?*
- *What is their occupation?*
- *What is their job title?*
- *What are their values?*
- *What is their lifestyle?*
- *How loyal are they?*
- *Where would they buy the brand?*
- *How would they buy the brand?*

Key question: How do you make the world a better place?
- *What do you do?*
- *Why do you do it?*
- *Is it sustainable and how?*
- *How did the organization start?*
- *Who are the people behind its success and what are they like?*
- *What have been the major events to date?*

Key question: What is it like to work for your organization?
- *How big is the organization?*
- *How many people does it employ?*
- *Does it make a profit?*
- *How big a market share do you have?*

- ▶ *Is the organization competitive?*
- ▶ *How does the quality of the products or services compare with your competitors?*
- ▶ *Has the organization used advertising or marketing?*
- ▶ *Do the founders or organization share ethical or environmental views?*
- ▶ *What issues could cause the brand to fail?*
- ▶ *What is the common public perception of this type of organization?*
- ▶ *Are there industry bodies such as unions, pressure groups or trade journals that represent this type of organization and what is their view?*
- ▶ *Do all concerned parties share the same point of view?*
- ▶ *Which matters are contentious?*
- ▶ *Is training and development offered to staff?*
- ▶ *Are staff rewarded for their performance?*
- ▶ *Are staff proud of their role in the organization?*
- ▶ *Is there a distinct hierarchical relationship between staff?*
- ▶ *Does the organization practise what it preaches?*
- ▶ *Is there any friction between departments?*
- ▶ *Is there a code of good manners? Polite, rude or ambivalent?*
- ▶ *Are staff helpful?*
- ▶ *If the organization has more than one office, are there different attitudes from location to location?*
- ▶ *What unites the organization's people?*

Key question: Can you express your business vision for five years' time?
- ▶ *What is your aim?*
- ▶ *How will you know if you have succeeded?*
- ▶ *If you could dream anything, what would it be?*
- ▶ *What would you like this brand to be remembered for?*

Key question: What would you avoid or include when describing your company?
- ▶ *What are the most important points to remember?*
- ▶ *Are there any phrases or words to describe the company or marketplace that should be avoided?*

Key question: Can you describe your business in a single sentence?

▶ *Could you describe your organization, product or service to a child?*

ANALYSIS AND INTERPRETATION

The brand team will analyse the research material and the answers from the question session. Their task is to identify the Strengths, Weaknesses, Opportunities and Threats (SWOT) for the future brand. The brand team will then formulate recommendations on the key elements of the brand criteria:

▶ **Purpose:** *The brand's purpose is _____*
▶ **Vision:** *The brand's ambition is _____*
▶ **Values:** *The brand stands for _____*
▶ **Mission statement:** *To be formulated with the management team*
▶ **Proposition:** *Our brand is the only _____ that _____!*
▶ **Position:** *Our brand's market niche is _____*
▶ **Personality:** *If this brand was a person it would be _____*
▶ **Audience:** *The brand's audience is _____*

The key branding criteria must be simple and clear. The brand strategy needs to be easily communicated and understood by all interested parties.

PRESENTATION

The findings, analysis and recommendations will be presented in a board meeting to the management team. The presentation may include audio-visual content, such as a projector or flat-screen presentation. Video or slides may be used. It can be more effective to use mounted boards to display key facts and findings. The most important point is that the presenter is confident with their chosen medium.

The presentation of the market research and questions is an important meeting. It is an opportunity to recall the purpose of the exercise and make recommendations on the findings. The presentation should be made to the management team, founders or leadership of the organization.

Following the presentation it is usual to answer questions about the proposals and findings. If any suggestions are met with reluctance then a follow-up meeting should be agreed at which these issues can be resolved. It is important to reach agreement and sign off the final brand strategy.

The approved brand strategy should be shared with the whole organization, as everyone has their part to play in the manifestation of the brand.

TEST YOURSELF

▶ *What is a brand purpose?*

▶ *What is a brand vision?*

▶ *What are brand values?*

▶ *What is a mission statement?*

▶ *What is a brand proposition?*

▶ *How do you position a brand?*

▶ *Describe a brand personality?*

Part three
Brand implementation

8

The importance of design

In this chapter you will learn about:
- *what good design is*
- *why design is an undervalued asset*
- *the importance of design in brand building*
- *global design centres*
- *the value of creative thinking*
- *design in business education*

Some of the world's biggest brands are defined by their use of design. Imagine riding on the London Underground without Henry Beck's tube map, drinking Coca-Cola without Alex Samuelson's curved bottle, or listening to rock music without Leo Fender's Stratocaster electric guitar. Some objects are so familiar that we take them for granted and seldom know the name of the designer, but their power in defining the brand is paramount.

What is good design?

Dieter Rams is one of the world's most influential industrial designers and his work for Braun, the German consumer electronics company, helped define the brand. In the 1970s, Rams became increasingly concerned with the problem of obsolescence and the throwaway society. Aware that he was potentially contributing to this issue he defined his ten principles for good design.

Dieter Rams' Ten Principles of Good Design

Good design is innovative.

Good design makes a product useful.

Good design is aesthetic.

Good design makes a product understandable.

Good design is unobtrusive.

Good design is honest.

Good design is long-lasting.

Good design is thorough down to the last detail.

Good design is environmentally friendly.

Good design is as little design as possible.

These rules are widely agreed in the design industry to be the perfect guide for good design.

When Dieter Rams joined Braun in 1955 most radios and televisions were housed in large wooden cabinets disguised to look like household furniture. He helped to reposition Braun with a futuristic functionalist style that benefited from new technology and materials. He pioneered an elegant industrial look in white, grey and later matt black. He standardized the size of Braun's hi-fi equipment which allowed separates to be combined to build a system. By 1963 he was appointed Braun's head of design and he stayed with the brand until he retired as design director in 1995. In 40 years he designed iconic products that included: the SK4 record player (also known as Snow White's coffin because of its clear Perspex lid), the ET44 calculator and the Universal Shelving System for Vitsoe. Jonathan Ive has acknowledged Rams' influence in his work at Apple, which includes the iPod.

Dieter Rams believes that the role of the designer is to question everything that seems obvious and describes his approach to design as 'less, but better'.

Undervalued asset

There is a tendency for the media to focus on a limited aspect of design and it is often portrayed through magazines and Sunday supplements as being focused on the consumer – fashion, soft furnishings and expensive luxury goods. The word 'design' is often used as a lazy prefix to justify a price increase: designer shades, designer suits, designer stubble! Creative software tools are available on nearly every personal computer giving the impression that anyone can be a designer. The combined effect can trivialize and devalue design and gives it a narrow focus on its contribution and yet it concerns so much more: experiences, processes, new ideas, creativity, efficiency, performance, sustainability and importantly, value.

The UK has long been celebrated for its creative contribution to the world economy. There are many different design disciplines, including graphic, product, packaging, interactive, retail, service and environment. According to government research, 'the global market value of the creative industries increased from \$831 billion in 2000 to \$1.3 trillion in 2005; more than 7 per cent of global GDP'. In 2006 the UK's creative industries made up 6.4 per cent of Gross Value Added (GVA), making it the largest creative sector in the world relative to GDP. In 2010 the London Development Agency revealed that the creative industries in London alone generate £21 billion or 16 per cent of London's GVA annually and is the second largest industry after the business services sector.

Creative courses are extremely attractive to students in the UK and 'Design Studies' was the UK's second most popular degree course in 2009. With the financial success of the creative industries and the availability of qualified design talent it is surprising that design is not used more in business, especially by small to medium-sized enterprises (SMEs). Only 19 per cent of the UK's businesses use external design consultants and 45 per cent have no design activity at all (*Value of Design Fact Finder,* Design Council, 2007).

Insight

The management guru Tom Peters has long advocated design as part of business strategy and he talks extensively about this in his book *Re-imagine!* Business magazines that champion design include *Bloomberg Businessweek* (previously known as *BusinessWeek*) and *Fast Company*.

Design in practice

Design is the medium that can most dramatically exercise differentiation. It affects everything from an insurance policy to the latest hybrid car and can transform processes, systems and organizations. Design can be used in every experience and should be looked at from a customer, employee and a supplier point of view. The greater the value that is placed upon design the more value it will return to the brand.

Too often design gets treated as something you do at the end of a job for a quick fix or tidy-up. It tends to be viewed as a final gloss solution instead of a primary concern. But design is not an add-on service, it is central to a business and its success depends on its full integration. Design is the difference that can provide the competitive advantage to distinguish a business, product or service in its marketplace.

There are typically four levels at which design skills are adopted by businesses:

1 **Amateur design:** *Design issues are handled by staff without any formal design training as design is viewed as expensive and not fundamental to the business.*
2 **Aesthetic design:** *Design is used late in the process to tidy up the appearance of a product or service and add a superficial gloss.*
3 **Project design:** *Professional designers are valued and they are an integral part of the project team from the start.*
4 **Strategic design:** *Design is an integral part of the organization's culture and is represented at board level.*

How design builds brands

Samsung

Before the millennium Samsung was best known for uninspiring budget consumer electronics that competed primarily on value alone. In the mid-1990s a dramatic shift occurred in the positioning of the brand. The Chairman, Kun-Hee Lee had been shocked when he realized how consumers in the US perceived his products and he was concerned that Samsung was losing credibility due to its pursuit of quantity rather than quality. He issued his vision for a new design-led future, which became a book – *Change begins with me* – and famously appealed to his employees to 'change everything except your wife and family'!

Samsung has a 70-year history that began with Kun-Hee Lee's father. Samsung was founded in 1938 and was originally an export business for dried fish! The name Samsung is Korean for three stars, which is considered an auspicious number.

(Contd)

Chairman Lee had previously studied in both Japan and the US and following advice from a Japanese design consultant he sent a delegation to the Pasadena Art Centre College in the US to instigate an internal design institute in Seoul. Gordon Bruce, an industrial design consultant, and James Miho, a graphic designer, joined Samsung from Pasadena to help set up the new design centre. The Americans soon realized that their new Korean students would not challenge their ideas as the Korean culture was too respectful and favours loyalty and obedience. This mindset is not conducive to questioning the *status quo* and breaking new ground in design. The tutors wanted the students to stop morphing other cultures and discover their own uniqueness. They had the foresight to see that the students would benefit from a global workshop to get a perspective on consumer behaviour and better understand their own nature. The Innovative Design Lab of Samsung (IDS) students were then challenged to find symbols of Korean identity that could inform the brand direction for Samsung. Korea's own sense of identity had been compromised by long periods of foreign occupation. The national flag proved to be a valuable source of inspiration. The South Korean flag has the *Tae Kuk* (yin and yang symbol) which represents the unity and duality of all things. This has developed into Samsung's design philosophy, the 'Balance of Reason and Feeling'. In an interview with *Fast Company* magazine, Samsung stated that 'reason is rational, sharp-edged and very geometric' and 'feeling is soft and organic – it makes an emotional connection with the user'.

This radical shift and investment in design has led to a number of high-profile design awards. Chairman Lee's design revolution was based on the understanding that you cannot differentiate by technology alone.

Interbrand, the global brand consultancy that publish the annual global brands survey, have recognized Samsung as one of the world's fastest growing brands and in 2009 Samsung was placed at number 19 in global ranking, compared with 2001 when they were placed at number 42. This position stands testament to their investment in design and their brave decision to shift from high-volume, lower-priced consumer goods to design-led products.

IBM

Thomas J. Watson Jnr was IBM's CEO during their most dramatic period of growth, between 1952 and 1971. He led the company from its origins in typewriters straight through to the computer era. Like Samsung's Chairman Lee, he was the son of the founder and shared a great belief in the power of design. He said that 'good design is good business' and believed that corporate image was essential to gaining public confidence. A strict smart dress code was expected of his employees and the corporate image extended to IBM's buildings which were designed by renowned architects, including Mies van der Rohe, Marcel Breuer and Eero Saarinen.

IBM employed some of the world's most talented designers and the famous American graphic designer Paul Rand created the IBM logo. Charles and Ray Eames, the famous furniture designers, created a series of promotional films, exhibitions and museum installations. IBM became known as 'Big Blue' and was renowned for its cutting edge innovation.

IBM maintains its commitment to design and in 2009 marked the 17th consecutive year that it had received more US patents than any other company in the world. Their total nearly quadrupled Hewlett-Packard's and exceeded the combined outputs of Microsoft, Hewlett-Packard, Oracle, Apple, Accenture and Google. IBM believes that 'design is vital to the success of most products and services. The visual and interaction design of the total user experience directly affects sales, service cost, productive use, customer loyalty, and almost every other aspect of doing business'.

Global design centres

Many Far-Eastern nations are building design centres as part of their national strategy to gain a competitive advantage for their businesses according to the 'Cox Review of Creativity in Business'.

South Korea has a 12-storey complex called 'The Korea Design Center' which has been built to raise national competitiveness through design. Taiwan also has a national design centre which is two-thirds government funded. Singapore's Fusionopolis creative centre covers 200 hectares and brings together entrepreneurs, scientists and researchers to interact and exchange ideas.

In April 2009, The University of Cambridge published the 'International Design Scoreboard'. The key countries which are taking design seriously include Korea, Taiwan, Singapore and China. In both Singapore and Korea, ongoing public investment is beginning to result in a clear design capability, which is evident through design education and the international registration of trade marks and designs. Taiwan already has 7,000 designers and this is increasing at a rate of nearly 400 per year. As well as encouraging design, Taiwan has invited technology companies, including Microsoft, Dell, IBM, Sony and Hewlett-Packard, to set up 'innovation R&D centres'.

China's municipal government has an ambition for design to be celebrated in its country and to change the world view from 'made in China' to 'designed in China'. The city of Shenzhen wants to establish itself as the 'Design Capital' of China and in 2009 has around 20,000 professional designers. Over the past ten years there has been phenomenal growth in design education. There are now approximately 130 design-related courses in 200 Chinese universities.

The UK has a global reputation as a centre for creativity and design and prominent companies choose to locate their design centres here, including Samsung, Panasonic, Nokia and Nissan.

The value of creative thinking

Creativity is a fundamental element of business success as is proven by successful brands like Samsung, Braun and Apple. Creativity is not an optional extra and cannot just be switched on.

SIR KEN ROBINSON

In his book, *The Element*, Sir Ken Robinson says that 'school systems tend to be preoccupied with certain sorts of critical analysis and reasoning' and there is a hierarchy of subjects with mathematics, science and language skills at the top, humanities in the middle and the arts at the bottom. Robinson says that schools have followed 'the academic culture of universities, which has tended to push aside any sort of activity that involves the heart, the body and the senses'. The result is that school systems have provided 'us with a very narrow view of intelligence and capacity and overvalue particular sorts of talent and ability'. He writes that 'academic ability is very important, but so are other ways of thinking'.

EDWARD DE BONO

De Bono is the originator of the term 'lateral thinking' which became popular after his book *New Think: The Use of Lateral Thinking* was published in 1967; he has since written over 40 books on creativity and thinking.

The Edward de Bono Thinking Systems have been taught to over 7.5 million students and children in over 30 countries and are now the most widely-used courses in the world for direct teaching of thinking in schools. Edward de Bono wrote the *Six Thinking Hats* in 1985 as a tool for group discussion and individual thinking. It provides a way for groups to think together more efficiently. The method has been adopted by progressive organizations including NASA, IBM, Honeywell and the British Airports Authority (BAA). The two main purposes are firstly to simplify thinking by dealing with one thing at a time (separate emotion from logic, creativity from information and so on), and secondly to allow a switch in thinking from a logical thought process which is to prove yourself right to something which allows creative new ideas to flow.

The biggest enemy of thinking is complexity, for that leads to confusion. When thinking is clear and simple, it becomes more enjoyable and more effective.

Edward de Bono

Design in business education

There are excellent degree courses in Design and Business but it is rare that they integrate. At postgraduate level this is changing: 'Design London' is a joint venture between the Royal College of Art and Imperial College London where all MBA students are required to take the Innovation, Entrepreneurship and Design (IED) course.

Throughout the world different departments are starting to work together so that MBA courses can teach the importance of design alongside other core business elements.

At the Stanford Institute of Design (or d.school) they believe 'great innovators and leaders need to be great design thinkers'. The d.school is a place where Stanford students from all faculties, including engineering, medicine, business, the humanities and education, 'learn design thinking' and work together to solve big problems in a human centred way.

SIR JOHN EGAN

Sir John Egan is a design advocate and one of the UK's most successful business leaders, Chancellor of Coventry University, Chairman of Severn Trent Water and a Vice President of London First. He was Chief Executive of Jaguar plc in the 1980s, transformed British Airports Authority in the 1990s and was President of the Confederation of British Industry from 2002 to 2004.

In an interview with the Corporate Design Foundation, he discussed how he valued design: 'Design helps to shape experience, and the quality of experience that people have of any company is the most influencing factor in shaping their attitude toward it. It affects loyalty, repeat purchase and the way people talk about the company to colleagues and friends.'

Sir John commented that in most companies design is the largest single investment that the board knows least about. Design budgets typically get chopped up between departments and handled in smaller packets where they are the responsibility of junior managers who lack strategic direction. He asserts that every investment in design should help an organization realize its vision or strategic purpose and advises that design is led from the centre of an organization and managed in a coherent way. Sir John emphasizes the importance of clarifying the brand's vision. Without a vision it is impossible to place design in the context of attaining the vision: 'Design is a strategic resource, and so must be organized and managed to provide the crucial link between business strategy and project activity.'

TEST YOURSELF

▶ *What is good design?*

▶ *Think of a brand which has been defined by its iconic design.*

▶ *Consider which design disciples would have an impact on your business.*

▶ *Which countries are investing heavily in design?*

▶ *Who coined the term 'lateral thinking'?*

9

....

Brand identity

In this chapter you will learn about:
- *the creative brief*
- *running a creative workshop*
- *brand names*
- *straplines*
- *logos*
- *mascots*
- *colour*
- *typography*
- *look, feel and tone of voice*
- *brand u-turns*

Creative brief

The creation of a brand identity requires specialist design experience and creative skills. The basic elements of the brand identity include: name, strapline, logo, colour and typography. A brand identity will also be expressed through its use of language, tone of voice and the look and feel associated with its visual style. It would be unusual for an organization to have all of these skills available in-house or be objective enough to create its own brand identity programme. You may consider the following two options:

1 *Working with a brand team that can deliver an integrated service for the brand strategy brief, creative execution and final brand implementation design.*

2 *Working with a separate brand consultancy whose skills lie in interpreting the brand strategy and delivering highly creative concepts.*

Insight

When choosing a creative team review their portfolio, research their reputation, evaluate their fees and then judge if the personal chemistry is good for a working relationship.

The creative brand team's brief is to deliver a brand identity that communicates the key criteria of the brand strategy (as described in Chapter 7):

▶ **Purpose:** *what the brand does.*
▶ **Vision:** *the brand's ambition.*
▶ **Values:** *what the brand stands for.*
▶ **Mission statement:** *how the brand is going to achieve its vision.*
▶ **Proposition:** *why you need the brand.*
▶ **Position:** *the brand's position in relation to its competitors.*
▶ **Personality:** *the brand's character.*
▶ **Audience:** *the people who are interested in the brand.*

It is essential that the creative brand team is briefed on the approved brand strategy, as these are the agreed principles of the brand. It is fundamental that the brand strategy has been established before any creative conceptualization begins. An attractive identity with no relevance will prove insubstantial and meaningless.

Creative workshop

The creative brand team will usually run a workshop with the client's management team to help find inspiration for the visual realization of the brand strategy. The creative process could prove strange to the management team and they may feel awkward or reserved about expressing their thoughts and feelings. The team may use some creative thinking exercises to help unlock the management team's reserve and get the conversation and ideas rolling.

There are many different ways to run this workshop but our experience has found the following exercises most useful:

CREATIVE EXERCISE 1: POSTCARDS

We gather hundreds of postcard-sized images of every conceivable subject and style. We place them in a pile in the centre of a table and ask the management team to choose one that expresses their idea of their organization as it is now and choose a second one to describe how they would like it to be. This never fails to get some very interesting results. People who are not used to thinking laterally are encouraged to think in an abstract way. The answers reveal much about the individual and their view of the world. The exercise demonstrates how we all see things differently: some people choose an image for its literal meaning and others will choose an image for a metaphorical meaning.

CREATIVE EXERCISE 2: BRANDS

We ask our clients to talk individually about their favourite brands and what they mean to them. This is balanced with the brand that they most dislike and a reason behind their answer. These questions can be answered in any way, but it is important to understand what it is about their choices that each member of the management team really likes or dislikes. For example, is it the typeface, symbol, colour or is it more to do with the ethos behind the brand and a shared passion for what they stand for?

CREATIVE EXERCISE 3: SYMBOLISM

We explore the management team's feelings towards colour and its associations. We get our clients to think in an abstract way about what best represents or symbolizes their brand. The further use of the postcards can help as a tool to unlock the imagination.

CREATIVE EXERCISE 4: ON BRAND – OFF BRAND

This exercise is similar to a parlour game and forces the management team to consider how their brand would manifest itself in a series of abstract scenarios. The aim is to pinpoint what would be 'on brand' and what would be the opposite or 'off brand'. This type of exercise points towards the type of imagery that would be suitable in the event of an advertising campaign or marketing promotion to support the brand. It is effective at getting into the psychology of the brand and what it stands for.

The following scenarios are suggestions for consideration. We have provided typical answers from opposite sides of the spectrum to illustrate the type of response:

1 *If the brand was represented as a sport, what type of sport would it be? Examples include:*
    a *Football: accessible; anyone can get together with friends for a ball game.*
    b *Show jumping: requires expensive equipment, a field and a horse!*

2 *If the brand was represented as a test of your wits, what would it be? Examples include:*
    a *A newspaper Sudoku puzzle: accessible but with a hint of academia.*
    b *A card game of Poker: high risk with a hint of glamour.*

3 *If the brand were a breed of dog, what would it be? Examples include:*
    a *Labrador: a faithful companion and the most popular breed of dog.*
    b *Chihuahua: a popular breed with celebrities.*

4 If the brand were a tree, what type of tree would it be? Examples include:

   a Oak: tall, strong and long-lived; a national tree for the UK.

   b Palm tree: exotic and suggestive of sun-drenched holidays.

5 If the brand were a type of music, what type of music would it be? Examples include:

   a Rock: loud, rebellious and has attitude.

   b Classical: cultured and sophisticated.

6 If the brand were a meal, what choice of dish might it be? Examples include:

   a Fish and chips: one of the UK's favourite dishes; inexpensive.

   b Sea bass: expensive and considered a luxury.

These scenarios may at first seem a little strange but they can get a debate going as to what exactly defines the brand and best communicates the brand strategy. These methods can really help to get an insight into the management's expectations for their future brand. You may prefer to try some different scenarios.

CREATIVE EXERCISE 5: MOOD BOARD

This exercise requires the management team to bring to the workshop images or objects that they have collected that appeal to their idea of the brand. They can cut out magazine or newspaper articles or provide their own photographs. Some people will bring an object that appeals to them and can tell a story or reveal a connection to the brand strategy. These will then be discussed by the group and judged on their merits. The approved material will be gathered and either photographed or stuck directly onto a board (usually referred to as the Mood Board). This material becomes the reference for the brand direction.

Every brand consultancy will have their own unique approach to firing the imagination and generating ideas. The workshop is a valuable exercise and will help to form the creative brand team's concepts for the brand identity.

We advise that after the workshop a contact report is produced detailing the responses, findings and views. This should be signed off and approved by management before the creative brand team begin any conceptual work.

The next stage for the creative team is the conceptual stage, which will result in the presentation of the brand identity elements.

The basic elements of the brand identity include:

▶ *brand name*
▶ *strapline*
▶ *logo*
▶ *mascot (if relevant)*
▶ *colour*
▶ *typography*
▶ *look, feel and tone of voice.*

The creative brand team will prepare up to three conceptual approaches, which will demonstrate their suitability across an appropriate range of materials, for example applied to business stationery, a brochure, advertising and a website homepage. The creatives will need to convince the management team that their proposals can be practically executed, as the management team may be inexperienced at imagining how the ideas will be applied. The presented material may extend to signage, vehicle livery, merchandise and uniforms. The chosen concept may be developed before reaching final approval. When the concept is signed off, final artwork will be created and a guideline of basic brand identity elements is produced.

Name

A name is the first level of brand communication and so it is imperative that the choice is relevant and meaningful to the brand it identifies. Choosing the right name for your brand is a very important challenge. Expectant parents get nine months to consider the name for their newborn child. If you have been in this situation you will know that family politics can have an influence. Do you honour a grandparent or other relative by using their name? How does the choice of name sound combined with your surname? Some names are fine for a child but how will they sound on an adult? Try imagining your child in a fabulous career and then consider if your choice of name will suit the position. Most names tell us a lot about the parents and their background: Apple, Moon Unit and Zowie are examples chosen by celebrity parents. It's the same dilemma with your brand; you want to choose a name for your brand that will give it a great start and increase its chances of future success.

Naming professionals are familiar with the origins of words, their esoteric meaning and emotional connection. They will be aware of clichés and foreign language issues and will be experienced at trade-marking the name. Graphic designers will contribute by evaluating the word in terms of its visual style. This is very important because a name is often seen and read but not heard. How will the word appear in black and white on a printed page or on screen? How will the name sound out loud? Some words are soft on the ear and others are abrasive or abrupt and others are just fun to say. An experienced naming professional will steer the suggestions away from cultural collisions when words translate as either offensive or ridiculous.

Your choice of brand name should reflect your brand values, be memorable, unique and easy to pronounce. Since the mid-1990s the internet has become an important consideration for naming: will your choice of name be available as an internet domain? This is the unique address that identifies your website and email. The scramble for a prestigious '.com' or '.co.uk' internet domain name has created a dubious market for so called 'cyber squatters'. These are people who anticipate the popularity of certain words and even register existing brand names to sell on at a profit. The internet is responsible for a wave of creative names driven by the desire to register a short name as a premium-level domain address. This tends to take the shape of the combination of two previously unconnected words to create a new name. Names for brands do come in fashions, like children's' names, but we don't advise that you follow a trend as you may find your brand dates quickly.

The choice of name will be at the centre of your brand strategy and will be the first thing people hear or read. Consider how your brand name will look in a newspaper story or magazine article stripped of its identity and reduced to a naked word in black type on the printed page – will it still communicate the brand? Of all the brand identity elements, your name is the least likely to change. Your choice of colour, logo and image may develop over time, but your name will most likely remain constant. A successful name is easy to remember, pronounce and spell and should complement the culture of the business. It will look good on the printed page or in an e-mail signature. If you get the right name it will be a valuable marketing tool that will literally be shared by word-of-mouth.

Creating a new brand for an existing organization is a harder brief than creating a new brand for a start-up business because they tend to come with a legacy of associations. Consider your budget and deadline and if there will be a launch or a gradual rollout. A new name must improve the public perception and recognition of the changed organization.

When do you need a new name?

- ▶ *Start-up: new organization, product or service.*
- ▶ *Business failure: if the existing name is associated with bad performance, disreputable behaviour and failure it may be time to consider a name change.*
- ▶ *International markets: growth into new geographical locations where the old name would be unsuitable.*
- ▶ *Acquisition: an organization may acquire other businesses or be acquired by a larger organization, and will need a new name to reflect the nature of the new business.*

TYPES OF NAME

Family names

The family name will be intrinsically linked with the business owner and if the brand is later sold the name may have the disadvantage of being linked to that individual or family. The new brand owner may then need to invest in a rebranding exercise if the name is not relevant to them.

Family name brands include: Guinness, Sainsbury's, Dyson, WHSmith, John Lewis and Robert Dyas.

Descriptive names

Descriptive names can be used to describe the brand promise and indicate the business purpose. The more descriptive the name, the more clearly it communicates to the customer, but this strategy lacks emotion and may limit future growth if the brand develops into different areas of trade.

Descriptive name brands include: Toys R Us, Homebase, Pizza Hut and Allied Carpets.

Invented names
Made-up words can be easier to copyright but may take time
to establish, as you need time to introduce the name and create
awareness. The use of an unusual spelling to create a unique
name is a popular direction but may confuse new customers
when searching online. Made-up names can be fun to use and are
attention grabbing. They are amongst the strongest of all brand
names and are suited to trade-marking and are easier to register
as internet domains. A made-up name may also be referred to as a
neologism – a newly coined word that is in the process of adoption
for common use.

Invented name brands include: Kangol, Karrimor, Lego and
Diageo.

Symbolic names
The use of a metaphor is a simple and effective way to project
the values of the business. Symbolic names link the essence of the
brand to a familiar metaphor. A symbolic name will not provide
an exact explanation of what the brand does but it does convey
the spirit of the product or service. The chosen symbol can lend
its values and associations to give a sense of feeling for the
brand.

Symbolic name brands include: Mongoose, Penguin, Jaguar
and Puma.

Abbreviated names
Acronyms or initials may be used to identify a brand but such a
name can suffer from anonymity without a concerted awareness
programme. It is a popular strategy with smaller businesses to
place their name at the front of an alphabetical list, e.g. 'ABC
Mechanics', but this can appear generic and meaningless. Successful
examples usually benefit from repeated publicity and exposure.

Abbreviated name brands include: NASA (National Aeronautics
and Space Administration), NHS (National Health Service) and
BMW (Bayerische Motoren Werke).

Geographical names

This type of name will always be associated with the region the name is borrowed from. If the region suffers a loss of reputation it will create negative associations for the brand. The best examples borrow the characteristics of the region to create authenticity around the brand.

Geographical name brands include: West Cornwall Pasty Company and Dorset Cereals.

Foreign-sounding names

Some brands use names to evoke a geographic region or suggest a convincing parentage. Some brands adopt this strategy with a knowing wink and a cheeky attitude.

Foreign-sounding name brands include:

- ▶ **Gü** *and its sibling brand* **Frü:** *these are continental sounding names for indulgent puddings inspired by their British founder James Averdieck's love of Belgian Chocolates. The umlauts on the ü create a happy contented smile!*
- ▶ **Häagen-Dazs:** *the ice cream brand was founded in New York in 1961 by Reuben Mattus who chose the Scandinavian sounding name to reflect the European traditions and craftsmanship that he admired.*
- ▶ **Möben:** *the British kitchen brand chose the name to convey the build quality associated with German products.*
- ▶ **Berghaus:** *the outdoor equipment brand started life as the LD Mountain Centre in Newcastle. The owners Peter Lockey and Gordon Davison spotted a gap in the market for quality equipment and began designing their own. Their German choice of name is a literal translation of the words 'Mountain Centre'.*
- ▶ **Pret A Manger:** *the British sandwich brand's name is French for 'ready to eat' and is based on the French phrase* prêt à porter *('ready-to-wear'). One of the co-founders Julian Metcalfe later founded Itsu, the Japanese-sounding sushi bar.*

Modular names

Consider the sub-brand or brand extension possibilities of the proposed brand name. A name may be used in a modular approach to prefix products and services to create a family series.

Modular brand names include McDonald's – they use the 'Mc' in their name to create a family of branded products: Chicken McNuggets®, McMuffin®, McFlurry® and of course Big Mac®.

Famous names and their origins

Adidas: The sports equipment brand began with two brothers who made sports shoes. They parted company acrimoniously following the Second World War and formed rival brands. Adidas is an abbreviation of Adolf (Adi) and Dassler (Das). His brother Rudolf set up his own brand Puma in 1948.

Epson: The Epson electronic desktop printer manufacturer's name simply stands for son of electronic printer (ep). Sometimes it helps to keep it simple!

Dixons: When the electronics retailer Dixons began in 1937, the two founding partners Charles Kalms and Michael Mindel only had room for six letters on the fascia above their shop window so they chose the name Dixons from the telephone book!

Tesco: When Jack Cohen started Tesco in 1919 selling groceries in London's East End markets, he acquired a big shipment of tea from T.E. Stockwell and customized the labels by using the supplier's initials and adding the first two letters of his surname.

Starbucks: The coffee shop chain is named after Starbuck, the coffee drinking young first mate of the Pequod in Herman Melville's novel *Moby-Dick*.

Haribo: The popular confectionery sweet brand derived its name from its founder's name and the German hometown of the company: Hans Riegel, Bonn.

Kangol: The hat brand was founded in Cumbria, England, in 1938 by Jacques Spreiregen. It derives its name from the K in Knit, the ANG in angora and the OL in wool – Kangol.

Lego: The toy brand of construction bricks translates as 'play well' in Danish.

Diageo: The drinks brand is the combination of Latin and Greek for *day* and *world*.

INSPIRATION FOR NAMES

- *Thesaurus*
- *Greek dictionary*
- *Latin dictionary*
- *encyclopedia – gardening, art, music, etc.*
- *wikipedia*
- *atlas*
- *music*
- *a trip to a book shop, library or museum*

Experiment also with the creative combining of words of different origin, and try to experience the product and environment from a customer viewpoint. Research the origin of the words to find interesting options. Sometimes the best names come to you when you are doing something completely unrelated!

Try literary devices, such as:

- **onomatopoeia:** *this is when the brand name sounds like the product, for example, Schweppes sounds like the gas escaping from a soft drink as the bottle is opened and it is also the name of its German founder – Schweppe.*
- **alliteration:** *for example, BlackBerry, Coca-Cola and PayPal.*

WHAT MAKES A SUCCESSFUL NAME?

- ► *unique and memorable*
- ► *easy to pronounce*
- ► *easy to spell*
- ► *has positive meaning*
- ► *has personality*
- ► *will suit future growth*
- ► *may be legally protected*
- ► *internet domain name is available*
- ► *fits with your culture*
- ► *fits with your brand values*
- ► *fits in your chosen marketplace*
- ► *looks good visually*

THINGS TO AVOID WHEN CHOOSING A NAME

- ► *generic names*
- ► *too many initials*
- ► *words that have negative meaning in international markets*
- ► *lack of available internet domain name*
- ► *limited growth potential*
- ► *tricky or unusual spellings that could lead to confusion*
- ► *don't use the founders name if you plan to sell the brand in five years time*
- ► *take care with long names that may suffer from unfortunate abbreviations*
- ► *never choose a name you could later be embarrassed by or find difficult to live up to!*

PLACES TO CHECK NAME AVAILABILITY

- ► *domain name search*
- ► *limited company name search*
- ► *trade mark search*
- ► *twitter search*
- ► *YouTube search*

TESTING YOUR CHOICE

Check the telephone directories and business lists to see how your choice would compare in your marketplace.

Answer the telephone with the potential new brand name to see how it sounds.

Handwrite a post-it note with the brand name and see if someone who is unfamiliar with your choice can read or pronounce it correctly.

Check the domain name is available first, before you become too attached to your choice. Your domain name needs to be short and easy to remember.

Does your choice of name reflect your brand values?

LEGAL ISSUES

When legally protecting a new brand, it's worth considering that names can be registered in different classes of goods and services. Ensure that your name is available for registration in your relevant categories before developing the brand identity. All considered names should be checked for legal and trade mark issues. Intellectual property lawyers can check that there are no conflicting business names in use.

Strapline

A strapline is a short memorable phrase that accompanies the brand name. It communicates the idea of the brand in a few words, typically no more than five. A strapline may also be referred to as a claim, tagline or slogan. A great strapline can become part of the consumer's turn of phrase further increasing brand awareness.

A strapline can connect with a consumer through an emotional proposition. It is a short sentence that distinguishes the brand from its competitors and encapsulates the brand ethos. Straplines are frequently used in advertising campaigns to deliver a brand message and may be updated occasionally to reflect the gradual repositioning of the brand.

A strapline can help to convey your brand values and what you stand for. If you have a name that is generic or has no meaning or doesn't clearly explain what your brand stands for, then a strapline can bridge the communication gap. The use of a well-written phrase can hit a chord with the consumer and will work wonders for brand recognition.

FAMOUS STRAPLINES

A great strapline can catch the public's imagination and create brand awareness:

Does exactly what it says on the tin

This is the famous strapline for Ronseal, the manufacturer of wood stain. It originated in 1994 for a series of TV adverts and the success of this strapline has been far reaching and the expression has entered popular use. It's simple, to the point, straightforward and trustworthy; the strapline is now a registered trade mark for Ronseal in the United Kingdom.

Other famous straplines include:

- ▶ **Audi:** *Vorsprung durch Technique ('Progress through technology')*
- ▶ **Gillette:** *The best a man can get*
- ▶ **Nike:** *Just do it*
- ▶ **Olay:** *Love the skin you're in*
- ▶ **Tesco:** *Every little helps*

QUALITIES OF A GOOD STRAPLINE

▶ *easy to remember*
▶ *short – around five words*
▶ *supports the brand's positioning*
▶ *emotive*
▶ *exudes personality and character*
▶ *unique and credible*
▶ *positive and not belligerent*
▶ *should not overpower the brand name or be mistaken for it*
▶ *can be legally protected*
▶ *does not repeat the brand name*

DO YOU NEED A STRAPLINE?

▶ *Will a strapline help your customers remember the brand?*
▶ *Does your brand possess a unique quality that is not communicated by the brand name?*
▶ *Does the brand name clearly communicate the brand's purpose?*

Logo

A logo is a distinctive graphic mark used for the identification of a branded organization, product or service. Throughout this book we have used the word 'logo' to refer to a brand's identifying mark. Through widespread public use, the word 'logo' has become the default term for any identifying graphic device, but industry professionals may use a varied selection of terms for specific meaning including: *avatar, colophon, emblem, icon, ideogram, logogram, logotype, monogram, pictograph, signature, trade mark* or *wordmark*.

LOGO ELEMENTS

The typical format for a logo is either symbolic (ideogram) or typographic (wordmark) or most commonly a combination of both symbol and typography.

Logo symbols

Symbols of identity have been used for thousands of years. Roman Legions would march under the symbol of the Eagle (*Aquila*). It was made of silver, or bronze, with outstretched wings. The symbol was so highly valued that the loss of the *Aquila* would bring dishonour to the Legion or signal its end.

The word 'monogram' is Greek by origin and means 'a single line'. Illiterate Kings and noblemen would identify themselves with a simple cross. The fashion for wearing signet rings is related to the ancient practice of validating a document with a wax seal. A monogram engraved stamp or ring was used to press its design into the hot wax to authorize the document. Monograms are often used by artists to sign their work, for example the signature of Henri de Toulouse-Lautrec was clearly visible on his art with a stylized monogram of the letters H T L inside a circle.

In the Middle Ages, a herald's responsibility was to identify knights by the unique marks on their shields, armour and horses. Today heraldry is a popular source of inspiration for trade marks. The car manufacturers Alfa Romeo, Saab, Porsche and Vauxhall all use logos that can trace their origins back to the heraldic age. These automotive examples usually relate to the region that the manufacturer established their business in.

The name Vauxhall is derived from Fulk's Hall, a thirteenth-century mansion overlooking the South Bank of the Thames. Fulk le Breant, a mercenary soldier who had been granted the right to bear arms for supporting King John, owned the property. His heraldic coat of arms featured the mythical griffin. In 1857, Alexander Wilson started the Vauxhall Iron Works Company close to the site of the old hall and he adopted the name and the griffin symbol as his company's emblem. By 1905, Vauxhall had expanded into automotive manufacture and moved to Luton, taking the griffin with them.

Symbols were first developed for an illiterate society as a means of identification. Public Houses in the United Kingdom are a great example of how a visual language was developed to express identity. King Richard II passed a law in 1393 that all inns should have a sign. An inn sign will typically face the street with a symbolic representation of the establishment's name – The King's Head, The Royal Oak, The White Heart, The Black Swan – each will tell a story, usually with a local connection. For example, the Marquis of Granby was a distinguished soldier who rewarded his retired non-commissioned officers with his sponsorship of an inn to manage. Not surprisingly many of these new landlords chose to celebrate his kindness by naming their inns after him.

Craftsmen of all trades have a long history of using symbols to authenticate their work and guarantee its quality. Marks were used to identify professionally accredited craftsmen or guild members. Early forms of trade mark were used by the following trades: ceramicists, stonemasons, printers, paper merchants and cabinet makers.

The success of using an abstract symbol to identify a business depends on the awareness of its relevance to the enterprise. In its most simple form, a fish monger would be identified by the symbol of a fish, a cobbler by a boot. Some symbols are familiar by their association to a trade but their relevance can be unclear. For example, a bookshop may use the symbol of an owl but its significance is esoteric. The use of an owl relates to the Greek Goddess of Wisdom, Athena, who was often represented as an owl – hence 'the wise old owl'.

Logo typography

A typographic logo is a unique setting of characters created specifically for the brand. The characters may be inspired by an original typeface but are usually custom made for the brand. The character space between the letters, their respective size and relationship are all fixed. These qualities make it harder for someone to copy or re-create the logo. The use of a standard typeface may appear anonymous and make your brand easy to imitate. The task of the typographic designer working on a brand identity is to create a letterform that suggests a style suited to the brand. Throughout the history of typography, letterforms have been designed to take advantage of the technology available. Type's original function was to transfer ink to the printed page and the design of typefaces reflected this purpose. Modern litho printing machines and the introduction of digital publishing have freed the type designer from many technical restraints. With the availability of font design software and vector drawing applications, type design has witnessed a revolution in forms and fashions. The legacy of type design has meant that certain styles of typeface will have associations with particular applications or periods of history. For example, the BBC has adopted the classic Gill Sans typeface for its identity and uses the typeface for their titles and graphics. The artist Eric Gill designed the typeface in the late 1920s and his sculptures adorn the outside walls of the BBC's Art Deco building, Broadcasting House.

The creative brand team can use their knowledge of typographic history to evoke certain qualities and bring elements of historical type design into the creation of something new for a brand. A certain typeface may refer to a trade or be relevant to the company or geographic area in question. A typographic logo is basically a sign representing a spoken word that is made of sounds. The typographic logo for the German consumer electronics brand 'Braun' is written in capital letters with a taller 'A' in the centre which visually accentuates the pronunciation of the name.

ALAN FLETCHER

Some of the best examples of type-based logo designs were created by Alan Fletcher, among the most influential of British graphic designers. He founded Fletcher/Forbes/Gill in the 1960s and was a founder of the design group Pentagram in the 1970s. His timeless and classic typographic brand identities include: The Institute of Directors (IOD) and the Victoria and Albert Museum (V&A). His design for the V&A is based on the typeface Bodoni. He helped established the Design and Art Directors Association in 1963.

A LOGO IS NOT A BRAND

If brand consultants make headlines it's usually connected to the cost of the logo. When a new public interest brand is launched, the national media will often write headlines like: 'New logo costs

X amount'. This has created a common public view that branding is no more than an expensive logo and brand consultants are well paid for something that – as is typically reported – 'the local school could have done better'! What doesn't get reported is the months of research, development and meetings before the brand takes shape and a logo appears. The logo is really the tip of the iceberg; it's the face of the brand that fronts a strategic system for brand delivery.

KEEP IT SIMPLE

The best logos are simple and easy to understand. We advise that a logo should work in any situation or media. Test the logo in black and white, at various sizes and photocopy it or fax it – will it still be legible and identifiable? How will it look on a webpage and could it be reduced to the size of a favicon? (A favicon is the small icon that is placed inside the internet browser's location bar and is also displayed on the bookmark menu. It has become a must-have to brand your website.)

Avoid the influence of fashions and trends for logo design, as they will date the design to a particular moment. A classic design will be timeless and can have the extra advantage of making a new company look as if it has some history. A sense of trend or fashion may be communicated through seasonal advertising and marketing campaigns. The subject matter should always be 'on brand' but the models or styles can pick up on contemporary trends. The best logos are exercises in restraint and reflect the 'less is more' school of thought.

Examples of logo design and their origins

Citroën: Two chevrons identify the French car manufacturer. This is a link to the company's origins as a gear wheel manufacturer.

(Contd)

Jaguar: The story behind the evolution of the Jaguar brand identity includes world history and a changing business model. The British luxury car manufacturer wasn't always known as Jaguar; it started life in 1922 as Swallow Sidecars for motorcycles. In 1926 the brand's founders, Bill Lyons and William Walmsley, began rebodying existing Austin Seven cars with attractive new coachwork and the business took off. In 1931 they revealed the SS1 Coupe at the London Motor Show. The car had been produced with the Standard Motor Company's cooperation and it is a point of conjecture that the SS initials stood for Standard Special. In 1936 the SS100 model was the first car to be sold using the Jaguar name. It was fashionable at the time for cars to sport bonnet mascots and an aftermarket existed with company's specializing in them. Lyons described an early leaping cat figure created by Desmo Mascots as looking like 'a cat that had been shot off a fence'. The famous motoring artist Frederick Gordon Crosby was duly commissioned to design the Art Deco feline that became the official mascot by 1938. After the Second World War the initials SS had a negative connotation owing to Hitler's *Schutzstaffel* and a new name was required. SS Cars Ltd had already been selling their vehicles using the Jaguar name and a certificate of name change was issued in 1945.

Montblanc: A six-pointed star identifies the luxury pen manufacturer. The points are rounded and when the star is positioned on the end of a black pen cap the white star resembles the snow peaked mountain of Montblanc – the highest mountain in the alps.

Toblerone: Theodor Tobler combined his name with the Italian word for nougat – *torrone* – to create his unique brand name Toblerone. The confectionery is identified by the symbol of a mountain peak representing the Matterhorn in the Swiss Alps, but look closely and you will see a second hidden symbol of a bear. The bear represents Bern, the Swiss town where Tobler registered a patent in 1909 to protect his brand and his father first began making chocolate.

LOGO GEOMETRY

First consider how the new logo will be used. For example, a logo that looks great on a business card may look awful on the side of a forklift truck. If the identity is going to be featured prominently on the surface of a product, then it will make sense to consider the space available. Most logos need to work well in a horizontal format, on business stationery – business cards, labels, compliment slips and letterheads.

We advise that the identity is worked up in black and white before applying colour. Imagine that your identity might be etched, engraved, stamped or embossed. How will it look without colour and reduced to an outline? There will be situations where the brand may be reproduced in a black and white newspaper article and a logo that depends on subtle graduations of colour will not stand the reproduction test.

Mascots

Aleksandr the Meerkat, Churchill the nodding British Bulldog and Ronald McDonald the Clown all have one thing in common: they are brand mascots. A character mascot can bring a brand to life with humour and personality and give a face to the brand. Mascots can create a happy and positive mood around the product or service. A character mascot is created to animate the brand's attributes or values and usually takes centre stage in advertising, exhibitions or promotions. Some of the best examples are institutions like the Sugar Puffs Honey Monster and Michelin Man of French tyre brand Michelin. Unlike a logo, a mascot can speak, adding a voice to the brand and giving an extra dimension of emotional connection. The choice of voice and its accent or tone gives the brand interpretation a deeper nuance. Churchill Insurance's nodding dog was originally voiced by the northern comedian Bob Mortimer and was memorable for his 'Oh yes!' catchphrase.

The insurance brand, comparethemarket.com uses a mascot brand strategy with a difference. Aleksandr the Meerkat is an aristocratic

Russian who is frustrated that his website comparethemeerkat.com gets mistaken for comparethemarket.com. This makes Aleksandr unusual, as he doesn't technically represent the brand he is associated with. The insurance brand has cleverly created an alternative website called comparethemeerkat.com to complete the joke.

Mascots have merchandising possibilities, for example Churchill nodding dogs are available from the Churchill website. One drawback of using a mascot is their tendency to require regular makeovers to fit in with current trends, for example the Michelin man has periodically been developed and updated since his origination.

The Olympic Games have an established tradition of mascot adoption since the 1972 Olympic Games at Munich when Waldi the stripey dachshund made his debut.

Summer Olympic mascots

1972	Munich, Germany	Waldi the Dachshund
1976	Montreal, Canada	Amik the Beaver
1980	Moscow, Russia	Misha the Bear
1984	Los Angeles, USA	Sam the Eagle
1988	Seoul, South Korea	Hodori the Tiger
1992	Barcelona, Spain	Cobi the Dog
1996	Atlanta, USA	Izzy the Whatizit
2000	Sydney, Australia	Syd the Platypus, Ollie the Kookaburra, Millie the Echidna
2004	Athens, Greece	Athena and Phevos based on dolls of Gods
2008	Beijing, China	Beibei the Fish, Jingjing the Panda, Huanhuan the Olympic Flame, Yingying the Antelope and Nini the Swallow
2012	London, UK	Wenlock and Mandeville

The two mascots for the London 2012 Olympics are called Wenlock and Mandeville. Their names are based on locations linked to the Olympics, Much Wenlock is the Shropshire village that hosted the first ever modern Olympic Games in 1850 and Stoke Mandeville Hospital was the birthplace of the Paralympic Games. The story of their origin is based on the last two droplets of steel from the construction of the Olympic stadium. Their design includes a hint of London with their Black Cab inspired yellow lights crowning their heads, and Wenlock wears Olympic rings as friendship bands. The three peaks on Wenlock's head represent the champion's podium and Mandeville's head crest represents the Agitos – the three crescents from the paralympic logo. The one-eyed characters are cheeky and playful and the brief for the creative agency Iris was to create mascots that would excite and inspire young people and encourage them to get involved in sport. An animation accompanies the duo with a story written by the popular children's author Michael Morpurgo.

In 2006 Javier Mariscal the Spanish artist and designer created the mascot for the Barcelona 1992 Olympic Games. The character was a dog named Cobi, who has since gained much admiration but was initially viewed with disbelief. Javier Mariscal is reported to have said, 'It is hard to fall in love at first sight with a dog that looks as if he has been run over by a heavy goods vehicle'!

Designing a successful mascot is far from easy and getting it wrong will attract a lot of negative publicity. But examples like the Michelin man, also known as Bibendum, can prove enduringly popular and central to the brand's image. Bibendum is over 100 years old and has made honorary guest appearances in an Asterix book and the 2010 Oscar winning animated short film *Logorama* by Nicolas Schmerkin where two Bibendums appear as policemen.

Colour

Colour is a valuable and powerful brand asset and its choice can be both symbolic and personal. We use colour to express our feelings, our emotions, political allegiance, social status and personal taste. Today we take colour reproduction for granted, but the story of colour is linked to trade, enterprise and technology. Nature is filled with colour but it is only relatively recently that we have been able to mass reproduce a spectrum of colours through print, inks and dyes.

Some colours are linked to prestige because they were originally difficult or expensive to reproduce and only the wealthy or ruling elite could afford them. The Aztecs made a red dye from the crushed dried bodies of cochineal beetles; it required thousands of the insects to create a pound of dye and it was offered in tribute to their rulers. After the Spanish conquistador Cortés made his expedition to Mexico in 1519 he recognized the potential for the Aztec red dye and carried it back to Europe. The Spanish had a trade monopoly on the colouring and kept its origins a secret. Consequently it was available at a premium and its dyed fabrics were enjoyed by the rich and elite. Cochineal remained the main source of red dye until the 1850s when cheap synthetic dyes became available.

Children are passionate about their favourite colours; anyone with children will tell you how siblings will squabble over McVitie's chocolate Penguin biscuits for the sake of their favourite wrapper colour. Colour can make the difference in the fashion business between a sale and a garment being left on the rail. Companies like Uniqlo (the Japanese leisure-clothing brand) and Brora (the Scottish cashmere brand) make colour variety their unique selling point. The Uniqlo 2010 campaign advertises 88 different colours.

So how do you choose a colour for success? One thing is for certain, be careful about turning to the world of fashion. Choosing a colour because it is the latest trend may date your business quickly. Your choice of colour should be fixed to a strong idea about the brand. Colour is a powerful marketing tool and colour recognition is immediate. It can connect an audience to a brand faster than the logo or written word, for example, IBM is often called 'Big Blue'. An unpopular colour like Brown can be turned into an advantage and become a success story, for example, UPS (United Parcel Service) is closely associated with the colour brown, with its uniquely liveried vehicles and staff uniforms. You can spot a UPS delivery van in busy traffic by its prominent brown colour scheme. Through familiarity a brand will become linked to its colour palette.

The creative brand team will be responsible for selecting a colour palette that can be implemented consistently across a wide range of materials, from printed brochures to sign-written vinyls, onscreen displays and websites. Maintaining a consistent colour match between these different mediums requires specialist knowledge and experience. A key colour may be chosen as the predominant hue but will typically include a secondary colour or a supplementary selection of colours to form a brand palette. These supplementary colours may be used to denote a hierarchy of products or services and communicate meaning through colour coding. When a brand is closely associated with a colour palette it will increase awareness of the brand and aid recognition.

WHY IS COLOUR IMPORTANT IN BRANDING?

▶ *Colour is linked with emotion and sensation.*
▶ *Colours have a strong psychological connection.*
▶ *Colour has a significant influence in purchasing decisions.*
▶ *We recognize a colour before we read a word.*

Insight
We surveyed the FTSE 100 companies in October 2009 and 52 per cent had a blue identity!

A general guide to colour

Before choosing a colour palette for your brand identity it is wise to consider the cultural and subliminal implications of a colour and how it is used in everyday language. Colour can provide inspiration for a brand identity and give deeper meaning to the realization of the brand strategy.

The following information is a general introduction to colour and its associations:

RED ASSOCIATION

Red is an emotional colour that conveys feelings of pride, passion, lust, sex, strength, energy, blood and war. Red is often used in national flags and football teams and is the colour of the British Labour Party. A red-letter day is a saint's day or holiday day as denoted on a calendar in red ink. It is an assertive colour popular with car manufacturers to display their performance vehicles. It is a strong and highly visible colour that is used for communicating important signals, for example, traffic signs and brake lights. Negative associations of red include bloodletting, fury, rage and violence. In China the colour red is considered auspicious and is found everywhere during Chinese New Year, at family gatherings and special holidays. Red is the colour of Communism and the Chinese government.

Scientists at the University of Plymouth and Durham University conducted a study into the psychological responses to colour. They observed that colour could influence the results of competitive sports. Following a study of the European cup results, they concluded that the most successful football teams played in red as either their main strip or away strip. The universities studied the league results for football from 1946 to 2003. Teams playing in red held the best home record and three of the world's most successful football clubs are Liverpool, Manchester United and Arsenal, who all famously play in red.

The luxury shoe designer Christian Louboutin uses the colour red for dramatic effect. It is the distinguishing characteristic that differentiates his shoes from other luxury footwear brands. He noticed his secretary painting her nails red and used the varnish to paint the sole of a new shoe he was working on. Now, celebrities like Angelina Jolie, Heidi Klum and Oprah Winfrey can be seen wearing his designs.

Red language
▶ *red roses*
▶ *the red planet (Mars)*
▶ *see red*
▶ *red book*
▶ *Red Army*
▶ *red-letter day*
▶ *red light district*
▶ *red handed*
▶ *paint the town red*

Famous brands using red
▶ *HSBC*
▶ *Coca-Cola*
▶ *Virgin*
▶ *Marlboro (sponsor of red Formula 1 motor racing brand Ferrari)*
▶ *Vodafone (sponsor of red Formula 1 motor racing brand McLaren)*

ORANGE ASSOCIATION

The colour is named after the Spanish word for the orange citrus fruit – *naranja*. It is believed that the name was first recorded in English use at the Tudor court of King Henry Vlll. The Old English word for orange is *geoluhread*, which literally translates as 'yellow-red'.

In the Netherlands the colour orange is a national colour closely associated with both the royal family and its football team. The national football team is known as *oranje* and wears an orange kit. *Oranjegekte* ('orange craze') describes the way Dutch people celebrate the Queen's Day or national football successes. During these celebrations orange becomes the dominant colour and is displayed in street decoration, flags, pennants and clothing.

Orange has a spiritual significance and is the colour of saffron robes worn by Buddhist monks. In Ireland the colour orange is associated with Protestantism through William of Orange the protestant English King (1689–1702), who won the battle of the Boyne in 1690.

In autumn the colour orange represents the festival of Halloween and autumn leaves turning golden brown.

Marc Newson the Australian furniture and product designer unveiled the Ford 021c concept car at the 1999 Tokyo motor show. 021c is the colour reference number for Pantone's most popular orange. The simple toy-like shape of the car was contrasted with radical details and a striking use of orange paint work.

The painter Edvard Munch was haunted by family tragedy as he lost his mother and a sister when young due to tuberculosis. His vivid painting 'The Scream' uses a red and orange sky to create tension and anxiety.

Orange language
- *It is widely accepted that no English word will rhyme with orange*
- *A Clockwork Orange*
- *Chocolate Orange*
- *Orange County*
- *orange juice (OJ)*
- *orange tan*

Famous brands using orange
- *Orange*
- *easyJet*
- *Sainsbury's*
- *GlaxoSmithKline (GSK)*
- *Tango (soft drink brand owned by Britvic)*

YELLOW ASSOCIATION

The colour yellow evokes the warmth of the sun and is the brightest colour to the human eye. It is symbolic of youth, fun and happiness. It has associations with spring, new life and the Christian festival of Easter. The yellow of gold is used to symbolize achievement, marriage, royalty and wealth. A gold medal is the Olympics' highest sporting award but, paradoxically, yellow is linked with cowardice and illness, for example, 'yellow belly' and 'yellow jaundice'. It is the colour of the desert sands, autumn leaves and bile.

The practice of wearing a yellow ribbon symbolizes the absence of a loved one. This is the significance of the 1949 John Ford western *She Wore a Yellow Ribbon* starring John Wayne. The ribbon's significance also inspired the 1973 pop hit 'Tie a yellow ribbon round the old oak tree'.

Yellow is a regal colour in Chinese culture and dates back to the Emperor Huangdi, known as the Yellow Emperor, who is credited with the invention of Chinese medicine. The Yellow River is widely believed to be the cradle of Chinese civilization and the river gains its name from the rich in yellow ochre tinted silt.

The Lonsdale Boxing Brand is named after Hugh Cecil Lowther, 5th Earl of Lonsdale. He was an extrovert character and a sports patron who was fondly known as the Yellow Earl and was the first president of the Automobile Association (the AA), a prominent yellow brand.

The Tour de France cycle race is famous for the yellow jersey, or the *maillot jaune*, as worn by the winner of the race since 1919.

The Yellow Cab Company of Chicago and Hertz Car Rental were both founded by John Hertz. According to tradition he requested the help of Chicago University for advice on the best colour to stand out in a crowd. They advised he used yellow and Hertz still use the same colour today.

Yellow language
▶ *yellow-brick road*
▶ *yellow jaundice*

- *yellow belly*
- *yellow fever*
- *yellow ribbon*
- *yellow jersey*

Famous brands using yellow
- *Aviva*
- *Shell*
- *Yellow Pages*
- *Hertz*
- *The AA*

GREEN ASSOCIATION

Green represents growth, nature, fertility and safety. Green is commonly associated with medical care, military, banking, finance and money. Green is associated with naivety, for example; being green or a 'green horn'. Green has a healing power and a relaxing quality that is easy on the eye. Green is a colour for action and a green light means it's safe to go, from emergency exits to pedestrian crossings and traffic lights. The origins of the green word are derived from the Old English word *growan* meaning to grow. Green baize is used to cover playing card tables and billiard tables because of its high colour contrast.

The green Libyan flag is the only national flag with no characteristics other than its colour, representing its devotion to Islam. Ireland is known as the Emerald Isle and the Irish consider green lucky. On St Patrick's Day its festive significance has reached the White House where the fountains have been dyed green. A green card is issued in the US to an immigrant giving them some of the privileges of citizenship. In Chinese symbolism, a green hat represents a cuckold, a man with an adulterous wife. The Green Man and Jack of the Green are symbols of fertility and renewal and are linked by association with the Green Knight and the folk hero Robin Hood who wore Lincoln Green. English people are superstitious about green and would typically avoid buying a green car or an emerald engagement ring.

Green's symbolism is internationally understood and it has gained political significance. The UK's Green Party promotes social and environmental justice. It was formed in 1973 as 'People' and changed its name to the 'Ecology Party', finally becoming the 'Green Party' in 1985. In 2010 the party leader Caroline Lucas became their first elected Member of Parliament representing Brighton Pavilion.

Green language
- *green-fingered*
- *green with envy*
- *Green Man*
- *Green Knight*
- *Jack of the Green*
- *green thumb*
- *green horn*

Famous brands using green
- *BP*
- *Marks & Spencer*
- *Lloyds TSB*
- *Greenpeace*
- *Waitrose*

BLUE ASSOCIATION

Whether it is cyan, indigo, royal or sky, more businesses choose blue than any other colour for their brand identity. Blue conveys trust and conservatism and is both cool and calming. It is a popular choice of colour with large organizations, from enterprise to the social sector and it is the colour of the British Conservative Party. It represents loyalty, strength, wisdom and trust. We live on a blue planet and it is the most abundant colour from the sky to the sea. In Western society it is typical for the parents of a baby boy to decorate his room in blue.

There are few natural instances of blue in foods and consequently blue is not considered an appetizing colour. The popular Nestlé confectionary brand 'Smarties' introduced a blue smartie in 1989 and then withdrew them in 2006 due to concerns about food colourings. In 2008 the blue smartie returned with a natural colouring extracted from a type of seaweed called spirulina.

IKB (International Klein Blue) was the new colour mixed by the French artist Yves Klein who developed the colour with chemists and patented it. IKB was an expression of his work that included canvases and performance art. The architects Future Systems designed the Selfridges building at Birmingham in a flowing organic form. It features a skin made of thousands of aluminium discs set on a background of Yves Klein Blue.

Blue has not always been considered respectable. In the Roman Empire, blue dyed fabrics were associated with craftsmen, peasants and the blue-eyed barbarians who painted their bodies in blue woad before going into battle and used it to colour their hair. We associate blue skin with death and other less respectable associations include: blue language and blue movies.

Blue language
- *blue moon*
- *the blues*
- *blue print*
- *blue humour*
- *Blue Monday*
- *blue blood*

Famous brands using blue
- *Barclays Bank*
- *General Motors (GM)*
- *IBM*
- *Samsung*
- *National Health Service (NHS)*

PURPLE ASSOCIATION

The use of purple colour dyes for textiles has long been recorded in history and literature to signify wealth and opulence. Shakespeare describes the purple sails of Cleopatra's royal barge when she first meets Antony: 'Purple the sails, and so perfumed that the winds were love-sick with them'. Shakespeare's account was informed by the writings of Plutarch, a Roman era biographer. In Roman society Emperors made the colour purple the exclusive symbol of high office. Imperial purple had a reddish hue and it was a difficult and expensive dye to reproduce, requiring the collection of thousands of sea snail molluscs. Purple still retains its high status and regal association and the imperial robes worn at coronations by British monarchs are lined with purple silk velvet.

Since 1917, the purple heart award has been given to members of the US military who have been killed or wounded whilst in service. The award originates from the American Revolution when in 1782, General George Washington issued the order that unusual gallantry, extraordinary fidelity and essential service be rewarded with 'the figure of a heart in purple cloth'.

In 1856 William Perkin discovered a synthetic aniline dye. It was the time of the Industrial Revolution and the commercial possibilities of his new affordable dye led to a fashion for the colour, which consequently made him rich. He had considered naming the dye Tyrian Purple in recognition of the Phoenicians of Tyre who made a purple dye from the glandular secretions of the mollusc *Murex brandaris*.

In 1905 Cadbury adopted its corporate colour of regal purple conveying the message that eating chocolate is a rich and indulgent luxury. The colour purple is a Cadbury trade mark, which the brand is careful to protect.

Purple language
▶ *purple heart*
▶ *purple patch*
▶ *purple prose*
▶ *born in the purple*
▶ *shrinking violet*

Famous brands using purple
- *Liberty*
- *Cadbury*
- *Milka*
- *Yahoo*
- *Silk Cut*

PINK ASSOCIATION

Pink is associated with femininity and there is a noticeable trend towards the wholesale adoption of vivid pink to brand every girls' product, from Hannah Montana to Barbie. It is also the custom to paint a nursery room pink for a baby girl.

In the 1950s pink was the colour of Rock 'n' Roll: hot pink dresses and Elvis Presley, who drove a Pink Cadillac Fleetwood. Donald Featherstone, the American artist, designed the iconic plastic lawn flamingos for Union Products in 1957. The plastic birds came in two designs and graced American suburban lawns in their thousands.

Dr Alexander Schauss, PhD, director of the American Institute for Biosocial Research in Tacoma Washington, carried out research into the psychological effects of colour in the 1980s. Baker-Miller Pink, which is best described as a bubble gum shade, has the effect of calming violent prisoners. It has been used in police stations for its settling effect on anxious inmates. Dr Schauss described pink as a tranquillizing colour that saps your energy. American football teams have allegedly used this knowledge and painted their away-side changing rooms pink to their advantage.

The *Financial Times* was first printed on salmon pink paper in 1893 to distinguish it from other financial newspapers. Thomas Pink is the Jermyn Street shirt brand favoured by city gents and was founded in 1984 by three Irish brothers, James, Peter and John Mullen. Their name is reputedly derived from an eighteenth-century London tailor celebrated for his red hunting jackets, and owners of these jackets were said to be 'in the pink'.

The *Pink Panther* cartoon began as a title sequence for the 1964 Peter Sellers film of the same name and was so popular he got his own show. The Hollywood animator Friz Freleng created him and other favourites, including Porky the Pig.

Pink language
- *in the pink*
- *tickled pink*
- *pretty in pink*
- *rose-tinted glasses*

Famous brands using pink
- *Thomas Pink*
- *T Mobile*
- *Lastminute.com*
- *Smile (internet bank)*
- *Financial Times*

MONOCHROME BLACK, WHITE AND GREY ASSOCIATIONS

Black has many connotations: in Western culture it can be used to suggest fear, evil or death. Its imagery can be negative – 'blackmail', 'blacklist', 'black hole', etc. Black is a very potent colour that is used to evoke class, elegance and wealth. Sophisticated clothing is designed in black, for example from the 'little black dress' to the formal 'black-tie'. Black contrasted with other colours can make a strong impact as it can be used to make other colours stand out.

White is associated with innocence, purity, cleanliness, spirituality and goodness. Artists, writers and filmmakers use white symbolism to convey these attributes: the white horse, the white wizard, the lady of the lake etc. White is most often associated with purity and spirituality and the heavens. White is also associated with healing, hospitals and doctors. Graphic designers create balance on the printed page with the use of white space. In the West it is customary to have a white wedding to symbolize the innocence of the bride, but in the East white is the colour of funerals.

Grey is a neutral colour, it is the middle ground between black and white and when we use the term 'grey area', we mean that something is not clearly defined. However we can use the term 'grey hair' to describe a mature person with wisdom. The 'grey pound' is an economic term used to describe the phenomenon of an affluent older generation. Grey is a neutral colour with no opposite and will complement any other colour. Silver is a prestigious colour which is popular with premium brands for its association with precious metals platinum and silver. The popular saying 'silver lining' implies that even in a difficult situation there is hope and optimism.

Black language
▶ *blackmail*
▶ *blacklist*
▶ *black hole*
▶ *little black dress*
▶ *black tie*
▶ *black ball*

Famous brands using black
▶ *Black & Decker*
▶ *Guinness*
▶ *All Blacks (New Zealand national rugby team)*
▶ *Black N Red*
▶ *First Direct*

White language
▶ *whiter than white*
▶ *Snow White*
▶ *whitewash*
▶ *white flag*
▶ *white wedding*
▶ *white dove*

Famous brands using white
▶ *Mont Blanc*
▶ *The White Company*

- *White Stuff*
- *Lillywhites*
- *R Whites*

Grey language
- *grey area*
- *grey hair*
- *grey pound*
- *silver surfer*
- *silver lining*

Famous brands using grey (silver)
- *Accenture*
- *Apple*
- *Audi*
- *Mercedes-Benz*
- *Silver Cross*

Colour checklist

1 *Does the appropriate marketplace have a common colour that consumers identify with this sector?*
2 *Does the choice of colour reflect the brand strategy?*
3 *Have international markets and cultural issues been duly considered before agreeing on the colour palette?*
4 *Has the chosen colour been evaluated for its effectiveness in the branded environment? For example: product, packaging, interiors, uniforms and vehicle livery?*
5 *Does the choice of colour have a close match onscreen and in print?*
6 *Will your identity work in monochrome and will it successfully transfer to grey scale or will it lose its legibility?*
7 *Will the choice of colour look dated in five years time?*
8 *Does the choice of colour have any connotations with the target market?*

(Contd)

9   Could the choice of colour palette be mistaken for another brand?
10 Will the colour palette aid recognition?
11 Will the colour palette work within the context of the built environment? For example: steel, chrome, wood, white walls etc.
12 Will the identity maintain its visual integrity at different sizes – very large or small?
13 Is the colour easy to manage across different media, for example will the colours match in print and on the web?
14 How will the colour look on different paper types? For example: uncoated stock is porous and can dampen a colour compared to a coated paper.
15 Have you considered the printed difference between cyan, magenta, yellow and black (CMYK) and solid (spot) colour results for your colour?
16 Have you compared different computer platforms for colour difference on screen? For example: Mac and PC have different gamma settings.
17 Are close-matching sign-writing vinyls available for your colour palette choice?

Typography

Typography is the art of the letterform and its discipline covers type design and type layout or composition. It is a valuable brand asset that can help to distinguish a brand and aid its identification. A corporate typeface becomes the handwriting of the brand and its style can convey character and tone. The careful selection of a typeface can communicate subliminal qualities about the brand, for example: youth, wit, seriousness, professionalism, adventure, boldness or sensitivity.

Many large corporations will commission a type designer to create a bespoke typeface for their organization, for example: VAG

Rundschrift, the round-ended sans serif typeface, was created specially for Volkswagen AG (the automotive manufacturer) as its typographic voice in 1979. It was part of a branding exercise to consolidate the growing group but Volkswagen no longer use this typeface.

Despite the availability of such a wide choice of typefaces, most businesses stick to a conservative selection of favourites. The digital publishing boom has meant that most people work with the typefaces available on their operating system and have never considered buying individual typefaces. This does have a bearing on the selection of a corporate typeface particularly in the age of email, PowerPoint and websites. The recipient of an email document such as a Microsoft Word file would not be expected to purchase an unorthodox typeface just to read the attachment. As a consequence the typeface Arial has become universally adopted by a multitude of businesses. However, there are many other choices available from the common set of operating system typefaces that can offer a level of distinction and character including: Georgia, Trebuchet and Verdana. However we do recommend that you consider the purchase of a corporate typeface for a bespoke brand identity.

HISTORY OF TYPEFACES

Johannes Gutenberg introduced modern book printing with his invention of mechanical movable type in the fifteenth century. He used a Textualis typeface for the Gutenberg Bible that was based on the gothic styles of handwriting used by scribes. As the printing technology spread, new forms of letter design emerged that reflected the tastes and fashions of the age. A Roman style of letterform was introduced in Italy that had more in common with the stone cut letters of masons. The Roman letterforms have influenced many of the typefaces in common use today.

The Industrial Revolution witnessed a boom in typeface design as new styles were introduced to sell products through posters, advertising and packaging. These ornate eye-catching designs are known as display typefaces and were mainly used for headlines and titles. It wasn't until the 1960s that there would be such a significant proliferation of new typeface designs, encouraged by new developments in technology and type manufacture. The desktop revolution in the 1980s had a similar outcome and type design continues to evolve with fashion and the relative low cost of type design software.

CHOOSING THE RIGHT TYPEFACE FOR A BRAND

Today there are a bewildering number of typefaces to choose from and few people can identify them all by name. Fashions come and go but it is important to make a choice that suits your organization and will be timeless. Choice is subjective but most people can sense whether a typeface is conservative, fashionable, contemporary, edgy, illegible or ugly.

Typefaces are organized into categories and typically will be organized by: serif, sans serif, slab serif, script, black letter, ornamental, clarendon, grotesque sans, humanist sans, modern, oldstyle, transitional and symbol.

The two most commonly referred to groups of typefaces are serif and sans serif:

Serif typefaces: Examples of serif typefaces include Times, Garamond and Baskerville. The identifiable characteristic of a serif typeface is the ends of the letters taper and feature tiny delicate strokes added to the tips of each letter. The general opinion is that serifs help guide the eye along the lines of large blocks of text. For example, the *Times* newspaper uses a serif typeface.

Sans serif typefaces: Examples of sans serif typefaces include Helvetica, Frutiger and Eurostile. *Sans* is simply French for 'without' and it describes a group of typefaces that do not feature delicate serifs at the tips of each letter. For example: the road signs used on British highways are written in a sans serif typeface.

We advise that you avoid complicated fussy shapes or fancy ornamentation that can distract the reader. Imagine the environment that the typeface will be applied to. It could be a supermarket, at an airport or for general corporate literature. Wherever you are, the written word must be clear and easy to read. The designer must choose a typeface that will carry the brand message for the lifetime of the brand.

Buying a typeface for corporate use can be expensive but a licence will be required to load a new typeface onto multiple numbers of personal computers. One option is to choose a typeface from the commonly available set on the Microsoft operating system. This is the most popular global operating system and will ensure that your emails, word documents and PowerPoint presentations will use typefaces available to the widest audience. We also advise checking compatibility with Apple's set of system typefaces. A complete list is easily accessible by checking online for cross-platform system fonts and this will ensure that your choice of typeface will be viewed the way you created them. If you choose a bespoke typeface the Adobe Acrobat PDF software allows you to embed the typeface in a portable document and share it with your customers without them needing to buy the fonts.

Be careful that you choose a typeface with the right style for your brand. For example, Comic Sans which is based on a handwritten style familiar to readers of comic books, does not have sufficient gravitas for most businesses but may be fine for a nursery or a primary school.

Both Trebuchet and Verdana were created especially for onscreen use and do not have their origins in the print industry. Classic typefaces were originally created for letterpress printing and their design and characteristics were intended for the transfer of ink to paper. Reading text on screen has different practical constraints compared with reading text on the printed page. Onscreen typefaces usually have a higher x-height in the lowercase, which improves legibility.

Newspapers and magazines are a good example of how to use a typographical house style to achieve a consistent, attractive and distinctive appearance. A typographic style guide standardizes a collection of typefaces, each used for specific tasks and makes consistent use of sizes, style (italic, bold, large and small capital letters) and the special characters known as ligature. The consistent use of a typeface will build recognition and help to identify a brand.

Considerations for effective typography

▶ *Upper and lowercase text is easier to read than capitals because the reader recognizes the shapes of the words.*

▶ *Regular upright roman type is considered to be more legible than italic type.*

▶ *Use contrasting colours when using colour type.*

▶ *Black on white text is easier to read than reversed (e.g. white on black).*

▶ *Exaggerated letter spacing and word spacing can compromise readability.*

▶ *Line length – wide widths of text are less readable than narrow columns.*

▶ *Restrict your choice of typefaces as too many styles can be chaotic.*

▶ *Serif fonts are more legible for large quantities of text than sans serif.*

▶ *Using a text grid gives a publication a consistent feel that aids the reader.*

Look, feel and tone of voice

The look and feel of a brand is the unique style that makes it recognizable, it is the subtle interplay of characteristic elements:

logo, colour, type, imagery, materials and use of language that collectively define the brand image. The strongest brand image systems are so recognizable that they can be identified or associated by their component elements alone. For example, if you see a Quentin Blake illustration it is hard not to think of the children's author Roald Dahl, and the photographic style of Mario Testino will always be associated with the 'Diana' brand of the Princess of Wales. Words can bring to mind brands too: the cake brand Mr Kipling will always be associated with the word 'exceedingly'.

LOOK AND FEEL

A strong brand doesn't have to display a logo to be recognized and can be identified by its behaviour and visual style. The work of artists and designers has become inextricably linked with the visual language of brands. The Smeg fridge, with its bold use of colours, and the Orange telecommunications brand with its use of quirky illustrations for its marketing material are both examples of the visual assets that help to identify a brand through its look and feel.

In 1917 the versatile talents of Alexander Rodchenko helped to define the look of the ideals of the early Soviet Union and his accomplishments included painting, textiles, sculpture, architecture, film, advertising and education. He became synonymous with the style of post-Revolution Russia and the Constructivist movement. He used a strong limited colour palette, typically of black, white and red, and his graphic posters were geometric, angular and strong in style. In the 1980s his work influenced a new generation of designers including Neville Brody and his work for the lifestyle magazines *The Face* and *Arena*.

A.M. Cassandre is one of the most celebrated of French commercial artists whose work from the 1920s through to the 1930s gave a style to brands, including French aperitif Dubonnet. His travel posters for train and ocean liner are instantly recognizable by their extreme perspective and celebration of the mechanical form. The striking and dramatic poster designs for Nord Express, Étoile du Nord and Normandie have become icons of graphic design and created a template for the future of travel branding that continues to influence designers today. Cunard, the luxury liner brand, uses stylized illustrations reminiscent of Cassandre for its 2010 marketing campaign.

The artist Jamie Reid gave the Sex Pistols band and punk rock a graphic look and feel in the late 1970s. His application of typography used cut-up letters from newspapers and magazines in the style of a kidnap ransom note. The cut-up typography method appeared on the Sex Pistols' singles 'God save the Queen' and 'Anarchy in the UK' and Jamie Reid's image of the Queen was later described by Sean O'Hagen of *The Observer* as 'the single most iconic image of the punk era'. Reid's strong graphic style became the template for the visual expression of the punk movement and was emulated by its followers.

In 1983, Paul Arden (the Creative Chief of Saatchi & Saatchi) conceptualized the famous Silk Cut cigarette campaign with Charles Saatchi. The campaign was based on a series of still lifes without pack shots, logos or text – just a sheet of purple silk with a slash in it. A classic example from this campaign featured a sliced loaf of bread wrapped in purple silk and drew on the visual similarities between the slices of bread and the tips of cigarettes in an open packet. The idea was so strong and the brand awareness so high that even the logo and type were unnecessary for its recognition. The same is true of the Marlboro brand which sponsors the Scuderia Ferrari Marlboro team. National newspapers have suggested that Marlboro allegedly avoided the outlawing of tobacco advertising in sport in 2005 when a bar code appeared on the Ferrari F1 cars – the bar code had a similarity to a packet of cigarettes. Following criticism Ferrari has since removed the barcode and replaced it in 2010 with a white rectangular outline.

TONE OF VOICE

Every industry has its own special words and phrases to describe unique practices or idiosyncrasies that are specific to its trade. This is called 'jargon' and can prove alienating or intimidating to an outsider. Anthony Burgess the author of *A Clockwork Orange* created his own vocabulary called Nadsat, based around Russian and English, to create an authentic culture for the violent teenage gangs in his seminal book. The film *Avatar* by director James Cameron uses a constructed language called Na'vi to give the indigenous inhabitants of Pandora authenticity. Consumer brands haven't yet created whole languages around their products but special words can be introduced effectively. The trade mark registered 'Frappuccino' drink from Starbucks is an example, and IKEA has created a whole naming strategy based on words with a Scandinavian feel.

A brand's special language can be a way of bonding customers to the brand. This is particularly evident in the category of youth culture where depending on the brand, a cult audience can be a desirable long-term marketing strategy. It could be a lifestyle activity brand like surfing, skateboards or music. These environments are host to a sub-cultural language that can have the effect of locking out some prospective customers. It is not just youth culture brands that use a special language, it could be the specialist hardware store where you want a simple widget but don't know what it's called and how to ask for it. How the counter staff help you can make or break their brand. Will they sense your discomfort and help you or will they enjoy your discomfort and make your life difficult?

A brand strategy is conceptualized in words: purpose, vision, values, mission statement, proposition, positioning and personality, but the expression of these qualities is predominantly driven through the visible elements of logo, type and colour. The brand vocabulary is often overlooked! Each working day employees receive hundreds of emails commanding their attention. How they answer these messages and write new ones should be valued as frontline branding. But how often do we consider if the messages reflect the brand strategy?

We advise that consideration is given to the articulation of the brand strategy in personal messages and client conversations.

The service industries usually excel at this, asking, for example, 'How can I help you?' instead of 'Do you need any assistance?' Some brands have a very strong attitude that manifests itself through every aspect of communication, for example, the Virgin brand uses a wit and irreverence with its advertising. In its campaign celebrating 25 years of Virgin Atlantic, the glamorous cabin crew dressed in red walk through a crowded monochromatic airport to the sound of Frankie Goes to Hollywood's 1980s hit 'Relax'. Two businessmen turn to each other and one says, 'I need to change my job'. The other replies, 'I need to change my ticket'. And then the headline fills the screen: 'Still Red Hot'. The advert is characteristic of Virgin's tongue in cheek style that is applied across the group.

Brand u-turns

Coca-Cola, British Airways and the Royal Mail are three brands that have all taken dramatic u-turns with their branding and returned to basics.

In 1985, The Coca-Cola Company took a big risk when it changed the recipe of its top-selling soft drink brand Coke. This marked the first formula change in 99 years, but it wasn't to last for long. Following a huge public outcry and reports that people were hoarding the original Coke, the Coca-Cola Company about-turned and brought back the old flavour now rebranded as Coke Classic. New Coke's reign lasted only three months before the customers reclaimed their favourite drink. The soft drinks giant has since introduced a number of variants including Coca-Cola Cherry and Coca-Cola Zero. The brand topped the Interbrand global brands survey at number 1 in 2009 for the eighth consecutive year.

In 1997, British Airways adopted a new livery for its fleet of aircraft that included customized tailfin art. The front of the fuselage featured a development of the typographical treatment of British Airways and a reworking of the older speed wing device into a new flowing red and blue ribbon. The customized tailfin designs became variously known as Ethnic Liveries, Utopia and World Art and featured artwork and designs that reflected the airline's destinations. The colourful tailfins attracted a lot of criticism and the former Prime Minister Margaret Thatcher famously used her handkerchief to hide the tailfin of a model 747 saying, 'we fly the British flag, not these awful things'. Virgin Atlantic capitalized on the controversy by applying the Union Flag to their aircraft livery. Tailfins are a valuable form of identification for air traffic controllers and pilots and the new liveries did not make recognition any easier. By the late 1990s British Airways adopted the scheme that had been designated to the Concorde fleet, the rippling Union Flag tailfin design known as Chatham Dockyard.

In 2001, The Post Office in the UK had a rebrand and, to much criticism, was renamed Consignia. The change had not been helped by choosing an unusual name and was compounded by the use of a generic symbol. The change was widely derided and the satirical magazine *Private Eye* ran a regular item inviting readers to spot lookalike logos. The rebrand was so unpopular that the Communication Workers' Union who represented the employees boycotted the name. By 2002 the organization became the 'Royal Mail Group Plc' with the following operating divisions: Royal Mail (delivering letters), Parcelforce (delivering parcels) and Post Office Ltd (managing post office branches and outlets).

TEST YOURSELF

▶ *When do you need a new brand name?*

▶ *Describe three different types of names.*

▶ *What are the benefits of having a strapline?*

▶ *Describe three qualities of a good strapline.*

▶ *What are the two elements of a logo?*

▶ *Name a famous brand mascot?*

▶ *Why is colour important in branding?*

▶ *What should you consider when choosing a typeface.*

▶ *Describe the look and feel of your favourite brand.*

▶ *Can you recall a famous branding mistake?*

10

Brand experience: touchpoints

In this chapter you will learn about:
- *brand touchpoints*
- *mapping touchpoint journeys for a brand*
- *the role employees play*

The definition of a brand touchpoint is any interaction between the brand and its target audience. The audience includes customers, suppliers, employees and shareholders. Each touchpoint is an experience that should be relevant to the target audience and reinforce the brand strategy.

Touchpoints cover every brand experience including the products, signage, retail environment, brochures, website, call centres, delivery vehicles, uniforms and the staff. The invisible touchpoints of ambience, atmosphere and attitude are equally important in defining the brand experience.

Each member of staff shares a responsibility to deliver the brand strategy, from the credit controller to the delivery driver. Their behaviour can influence the perception of the brand and their actions create touchpoints that affect customers, for example an incorrect invoice or a badly driven vehicle will reflect poorly on the brand. It is essential that each individual member of staff understands the brand strategy and is able to interpret it in relation to their role.

Touchpoints are the details that bring the brand to life and some of these details will be more significant than others. In order to evaluate which touchpoints are the most important, it will be necessary to observe and record all the typical interactions with the target audience. This will involve an understanding of their requirements and perspective. Touchpoints contribute to the brand's reputation, experience and expectation and are the practical execution of the brand strategy.

Mapping a touchpoint journey

The mapping of a touchpoint journey involves analysing all the possible routes the target audience makes during their relationship with the brand. It will require the collaboration of representatives from every department within the organization. All participants will be required to add firsthand accounts of how their contribution adds to the brand experience, before, during and after a sale. All the touchpoints should be of a consistent quality and aligned to the brand strategy.

To illustrate a typical customer journey we have created a fictitious travel company. Holidays are highly emotional experiences and exemplify how touchpoints are critical to consumer satisfaction. Many people spend months planning for their holidays and the rest of the year reflecting on them, so the experience is of paramount importance. People who take a package holiday place their trust and welfare in the brand. It's not just the destination but the company that is under scrutiny and the hospitality of the host nation. We may choose our holidays through personal recommendation, seek the advice of an experienced travel agent or arrange them ourselves.

The key touchpoints highlight the significant steps in the experience of the brand. Each one of these touchpoints will be rich with details that contribute to the overall brand impact:

TOUCHPOINT SCENARIO: PACKAGE HOLIDAY

A customer takes a package holiday by booking through a travel agency

A customer will typically experience the following key touchpoints:

> *Reads an* **advertisement,** *watches a* **television commercial,** *seeks information on a* **website,** *visits a* **travel agency,** *collects a* **brochure,** *speaks to a customer* **call centre** *representative, receives* **tickets** *in the post, arrives at the airport* **check-in desk,** *flies on an* **aeroplane,** *checks in at the* **hotel,** *meets the* **travel representative.**

Now let's take a closer look at the details within one of these touchpoints:

Touchpoint in detail: customer visits a travel agency

The prospective customer visits a travel agency to enquire about a possible holiday booking. The first appearance of the brand will be the street projecting sign that catches the customer's eye and directs them to the travel agency. The customer will then be aware of the branded external fascia of the building together with its window graphics and display.

As the prospective customer walks into the travel agency they will make assumptions about the professionalism of the brand. Is the environment clean and tidy? Does the décor reflect the branding? What's the atmosphere like? The customer will look around the travel agency and become aware of the furnishings and displays. Do these details complement the media image presented through the advertising and television commercials? Do these details confirm they are in the right place?

If the customer has brought their child with them, they will be grateful if the travel agency has provided a play corner with a selection of toys. Details like this can be tremendously significant to people with young families. Making a holiday booking and entertaining a three-year-old child can prove a challenge, so a small courtesy like a play corner can prove to be an asset. Even the choice of toys could be themed around holidays and destinations. The quality of the toys and the materials they are made from are noticeable details in communicating the brands ethos. If the travel agency provides crèche and play scheme facilities at its holiday destinations, it would be natural to expect that they would provide some form of entertainment for children, consolidating their position as a family-friendly brand.

The customer will expect to find a tidy brochure display rack with a plentiful supply of relevant brochures for the brand's most popular destinations. The walls may feature attractive posters of the holiday locations, which tie-in with the brochure display. If the brand is running an advertising campaign in support of a particular offer or destination, it would be expected that the visited travel agency is aware of the promotion and synchronizes its display around the offer. This may seem obvious but I am sure we have all experienced disappointing situations where retail staff are not up to date with nationwide campaigns.

The attitude of the travel agency staff will contribute to the brand experience. Advertising campaigns are typically filled with happy smiling people but this strategy will backfire if in reality the brand is staffed by disinterested unhelpful assistants. It would be natural to expect a welcome when entering the travel agency and an invitation to take a seat and discuss your travel plans. At this stage the customer will notice the furniture and the customer consultation area. The colour of the upholstery and the style and comfort of the seating are details in the look and feel of the brand. There are many options an interior designer can take when furnishing a retail outlet. Furniture can create a mood and express the brand in a subliminal way.

When the customer sits down to discuss their travel plans, they will be aware of the travel agent's working environment and the type of computer equipment they use. If the computer software malfunctions, the laser printer is out of ink or the internet connection is slow it could leave a negative impression of the brand. The ability of the staff to anticipate the customer's requirements and suggest helpful travel arrangements will affect the customer's feelings towards the brand.

Another factor to consider is the hospitality of the staff, for example are refreshments offered during the consultation and are apologies made if a long wait was necessary? These details may seem pedantic but they contribute to the subconscious brand experience and build on the customer's overall perception of the brand.

This travel agency scenario represents a detailed view of just one stage in the customer journey. The complete journey will take time and patience to map out as there are many details to consider at each touchpoint. The brand strategy is not just a theory, it must be realized through practical implementation – as they say, the proof of the pudding is in the eating!

Each touchpoint should be rated and scored from a customer's perspective. To balance this exercise it is advisable to compare each touchpoint with the brand's competitors.

Some touchpoints will be judged more important than others and resources will be directed accordingly. The travel agency example illustrates the possible stress points that can make or break a relationship with a brand. Any negative experience through any touchpoint can place a shadow over the brand's reputation. Think of any holiday you have taken and consider how a rude or unhelpful travel representative soured your experience. If the hotel was next to a building site it might have compromised a great memory.

If a customer is satisfied there will be a greater likelihood of a personal referral or a repeat sale. It is very easy for a customer to share their experiences with a wide group of people due to the popularity of social media (Facebook, Twitter, Blogs, Wikis, YouTube, etc.). Brands cannot govern these channels and can only influence a positive outcome by surpassing their customers' expectations.

Brand experience: employee

Behind every brand there is a community of people working together to deliver the finished product or service. The tools these people use and the equipment they rely on to do their job are all touchpoints related to the brand. A site visit to any company's premises can tell you a lot about how they value their staff. The choice of desk, the comfort of the seats, the brand of computer, the equipment they use, each item represents a choice. The quality of these items will speak volumes about the culture behind the brand. The equipment and behaviour of an organization can have a significant impact on employee welfare. As you scale a brand up to a large corporation the choice of tools and investment in working practices can have dramatic consequences. A faulty piece of machinery can affect the lives of thousands of people and have long-term consequences.

It is important that the employees are valued as much as the customers. In some organizations the outside view of the brand is extremely favourable and every touchpoint is expertly managed. We've all heard stories about household brands that have a great public persona, but behind closed doors it's a different story. It only takes one exposé by a journalist reporting on unhealthy working conditions, child labour, low pay, pollution and environmental damage to harm a brand's reputation. The pressure on touchpoints is to practise what you preach!

It is a challenge to get the touchpoints right for all your audiences, be they customers, employees, suppliers or shareholders. If you can get these touchpoints right you can deliver the perfect brand!

TEST YOURSELF

▶ *Reflect on a recent holiday experience and list the touchpoints from booking the holiday to your arrival at the destination.*

▶ *Now rate the touchpoints and put them in order of importance.*

▶ *What are the supplier and employee touchpoints for this situation?*

▶ *Look at the departments in your organization and record their customer touchpoints?*

▶ *What are the essential touchpoints for your daily work routine?*

Part four
Brand support

11

Brand champion

In this chapter you will learn about:
- *the characteristics of a brand champion*
- *the power of language in brand-building*
- *maintaining a high profile as champion of your brand*
- *creating a personal style*

What is a brand champion?

The Chief Executive Officer (CEO), the Managing Director or 'the Boss', whoever is in charge, is ultimately responsible for the brand. As the brand's champion it is their duty to protect and fight for the brand's success. If they cannot get passionate and enthusiastic about their own business, who will? The brand champion is the public face of the brand and is responsible to their employees, shareholders, suppliers and customers. As the brand champion they energize the workforce and inspire them to do their best. The brand champion must have the power to influence and motivate people, evangelizing their message so that the brand's voice can be heard. They are like the conductor of an orchestra, directing the organization in harmony through highs and lows but always towards a positive outcome. They will acknowledge and encourage their employees, excite their customers and lead with conviction and vision.

Characteristics of great brand champions

▶ *They have a passionate interest and understanding of the brand and a thorough knowledge of the organization around them.*
▶ *They are concerned with how the brand interacts with its customers, employees, suppliers and shareholders and are aware of their responsibilities to these audiences.*
▶ *They are at the heart of the brand strategy and ensure that it is clearly communicated, understood and consistently executed.*
▶ *They will be close enough to their customers to understand what they want and surpass their brand expectations.*
▶ *They will take a keen interest in their employee's welfare, building their self-esteem and a strong team spirit.*
▶ *Their own personal values will be in tune with the brand, delivering a business with honesty and integrity.*
▶ *They are aware of their limitations and will not compromise the brand.*

Great leaders are the embodiment of their brand. They live by the brand's ethos and will naturally follow its vision and values to deliver the brand strategy. They practise what they preach and consistently evangelize the brand. In an age of transparency, it's essential that brand champions are authentic, honest and have integrity. There have been some unfortunate cases of business leaders hiding aspects of their social lives that they later regret. A false image will eventually come unstuck and could prove harmful to the brand. The accessibility of social media makes any transgression an instant story, directing unwelcome attention towards the brand's credibility. Brand champions have enormous responsibility to the security of the brand and can elevate it to great heights or send it crashing down!

Insight
An excellent book on leadership is *Leading at a Higher Level* by Ken Blanchard.

If a brand is involved in a crisis, the media will be listening and watching closely to every word the brand champion has to say. Some leaders may not see themselves as brand champions, but when there is a crisis their face will appear on all the news channels. Whether it's a safety recall, a faulty component or an environmental catastrophe, at that moment the business leader is the brand. They will be scrutinized by journalists and judged by the public. The stock exchange reacts to business leaders' words and a successful brand will quickly lose its financial value if the brand champion doesn't say or do the right thing. In these situations the brand champion must communicate clearly and effectively. Of course actions speak louder than words and a crisis will need to be acted upon promptly in order to determine the brand's welfare. Brand reputation is a fragile asset that can be harmed by an unguarded moment or reckless behaviour. As discussed earlier, the phrase 'Doing a Ratner' refers to the moment in 1991 when Gorden Ratner devalued his jewellery business by £500 million in an unguarded moment. The CEO was speaking at the Royal Albert Hall to an audience of the Institute of Directors when he suggested that at 99p his earrings were cheaper than a prawn sandwich from Marks & Spencer and probably wouldn't last as long!

Business leaders have a duty of care to their brand's reputation. Brand champions need to say the right thing, do the right thing and fundamentally believe it!

Language

Brand champions are responsible for their words and must consider their rhetoric. Sticks and stones may break our bones but words can topple a brand! Language is a powerful medium for brand-building; we depend on word of mouth for the best endorsements. A conversation, emails, meetings and speeches, every word counts to support the brand strategy. A rushed email can have embarrassing consequences and humour can be misinterpreted when written in black and white. It is very easy for the wrong word to be used and an email can take on a completely different meaning and tone of voice to the one you intended.

Action

If you are going to talk the talk you must walk the walk and the brand champion is no exception. Visibility is extremely important and it is no good issuing orders from the bunker. An effective brand champion has a high profile and will be attendant at all the significant moments in a brand's history. Captains of industry lead from the front and stand alongside their troops in a show of goodwill and camaraderie.

When things go wrong, like a product recall or a safety concern, the brand's respective audiences will be watching to see how quickly the brand champion reacts, behaves and how they make amends. Actions speak louder than words and the brand's reputation will depend on the outcome.

Attitude

It is not enough to pay lip service to your brand and be seen in all the right places, you've got to believe in it. A brand champion must act with passion and conviction if they are to be trusted. When a politician stages a photo opportunity like kissing a baby, it is easy for the media to be cynical about their intentions. We expect our business leaders to be honest in their support of their brand or we will smell a rat! The genuine brand champion will do the right thing because they believe passionately in the brand.

Personal branding

Since the days of the Industrial Revolution, captains of industry have left their indelible mark on our perception of what makes a great leader. Their words and deeds still resonate today: for example Henry Ford's 'any colour – so long as it's black' and Thomas Edison's 'genius is 1 per cent inspiration, and 99 per cent perspiration'.

The world of commerce has witnessed some iconic characters that would stand out in any crowd. There is something about the role of the brand champion that attracts mavericks, people who think, act and even look different. Great brand champions have always been the very embodiment of their brand, from Isambard Kingdom Brunel and the Great Western Railway, Thomas Edison and General Electric, Henry Ford and The Ford Motor Company, Conrad Hilton and Hilton Hotels and more recently Dame Anita Roddick and The Body Shop. All are instantly recognizable and intrinsically linked with their business.

Sir Richard Branson, the CEO of Virgin, is famous for his casual look of open-necked shirt and goatee beard. Steve Jobs, the CEO of Apple, is renowned for his trade mark black designer polo neck and jeans. Anna Wintour, the editor of the American edition of *Vogue* is immediately recognizable with her perfect bob and dark sunglasses. These leaders all have signature styles that intrinsically link them to their brands. They have elevated their personal style into a significant brand asset. They can be spotted among the legions of the sober suited at any industry function and they help to position their brand. Personal branding matters, and if you look the part people will be more likely to believe in you.

Insight

For an in-depth view of an iconic personal brand, read Richard Branson's autobiography *Losing My Virginity*.

Audiences will be less likely to believe in the brand if the brand champion has a personal character and lifestyle at odds with the brand's strategy. For example, if the brand is promoted as fun and exciting with excellent customer service, but the brand champion is dour and introverted then the two identities will be at discord and compromise the brand's credibility.

To energize a brand and bring in a fresh perspective, brands may recruit their CEOs from outside of the business. The challenge is to appoint someone who complements the brand and can help it realize its true potential. When Sir Stuart Rose left the position of Chief Executive at Marks & Spencer's (M&S) to concentrate on his role as Chairman it was an opportunity to bring in new talent. Marc Bolland, previously of Morrisons and Heineken, was recruited to take over the helm of Chief Executive. This news was enthusiastically received by the stock market where shares rose almost 6 per cent and added £343 million to the value of M&S. Marc Bolland has his own personal urbane brand and has been described as James Bond, speaks multiple languages, dresses impeccably, drives a 1967 Aston Martin DB6 and has taken up shooting. M&S have chosen a brand champion to suit the brand.

TEST YOURSELF

▶ *Name three characteristics of great brand champions.*

▶ *Recall an incident where a poor choice of words has had a negative effect on the stock market price of the brand?*

▶ *Name a brand champion who has enhanced their brand through their actions and attitude?*

▶ *Describe three brand champions' personal characteristics and explain how they support the brand?*

▶ *Is your business leader an effective brand champion?*

12

Brand ambassador

In this chapter you will learn about:
- *celebrity endorsements of a brand*
- *product placement and 'the halo effect'*
- *how fans can act as brand ambassadors*
- *how employees can contribute to the brand experience*
- *external brand ambassadors*

What is a brand ambassador?

A brand ambassador provides a personal connection to the brand. We usually hear the term in association with celebrities who are appointed for their distinctive qualities that complement the brand. However, the least heralded but most important advocates are the employees who work for the brand on a daily basis. These brand ambassadors are the staff, who work at every level, from the management to trainees, who bring the brand strategy to life for their customers, suppliers and shareholders.

Celebrity brand ambassadors

Search for 'brand ambassador' on Google and you will receive a list of who's who in the world of celebrity, sport and Hollywood glamour. The title of 'ambassador' is typically bestowed upon the leading lights of entertainment and sport. The practice of product placement or the association of brands with famous people isn't new. In 1875 Captain Matthew Webb successfully swam the English Channel. He was the first person to do so and was quickly elevated to the status of international celebrity. His likeness was licensed to sell products and a brand of matches was named after him.

The business of watch-making is crowded with iconic ambassadors lending their cool to big brands. In 2010, Swiss watch brand Omega has a selection of celebrities, explorers and sporting champions to consolidate their image including the actors George Clooney and Nicole Kidman, the model Cindy Crawford, sailor Dame Ellen MacArthur and astronaut Dr Buzz Aldrin.

The cosmetics industry enhances its message with the endorsements of beautiful famous women. In 2010, the French cosmetics and personal care brand L'Oréal used celebrity brand ambassadors of all ages to appeal to their various target audiences including: Cheryl Cole, Penélope Cruz and Jane Fonda.

David Beckham, the distinguished football player and former England Captain, is often referred to as Brand Beckham for his astute ability to let his brand halo illuminate other brands. He has enjoyed a second career endorsing luxury brands and men's grooming products. He was the face of Brylcreem before shaving his head, the frontman for Gillette with designer stubble and an ambassador for Police sunglasses. His many endorsements have included Motorolla, Vodafone, Pepsi, Marks & Spencer and Adidas, for which he has his own signature-endorsed range of DB sportswear. At the beginning of June 2010, he signed a deal with Yahoo, ahead of the World Cup, allowing them to include him on their websites and products.

Insight

The halo effect: this is the assumption that success will attract success. The success of Apple's iPod primed the market to expect great things for the iPhone and that halo of expectation
(Contd)

has extended to the iPad. Celebrity brand ambassadors use the power of their success to attract interest in branded products and services.

When the Procter & Gamble brand Gillette appointed Roger Federer, Thierry Henry and Tiger Woods to exemplify the 'best a man can get' they wanted sporting champions to complement the brand's attributes of success, status, clean living and charitable works. Chip Bergh, President of Global Grooming at Gillette, was quoted by *The Times* newspaper in 2007 as saying, 'the three sportsmen support social causes and have reputations of true sporting values'. Thierry Henry stretched the definition of true sporting values when FIFA decided not to punish him for his infamous handball. The incident helped France qualify for the 2010 FIFA World Cup at Ireland's expense provoking widespread condemnation. Combined with revelations about Tiger Woods' social life, it illustrates the fact that there are risks attached to the use of paid brand ambassadors.

Fans as brand ambassadors

Trend experts will watch closely to see what the rich and famous are wearing. Even if they are not being paid to promote the brand, celebrities can endorse a product with their patronage. Steve McQueen lent his charisma to Heuer's Monaco 1133 Chronograph, famously wearing the watch in the 1971 film *Le Mans*. Variations of the watch continue to be sold by Tag Heuer today and the halo of McQueen's aura still touches the brand. He was also an enthusiastic owner of Triumph motorcycles and competed in motorcycle events. He asked his friend Bud Ekins to be his stunt double in the famous motorcycle jump scene from the film *The Great Escape* using a Triumph Trophy TR6.

Similarly, Ian Fleming's special agent James Bond sports a Rolex in the 007 books. In the Bond films, Sean Connery wore a Submariner model borrowed from Producer Cubby Broccoli. Bond was a fine ambassador for the Rolex brand, but had no official link with the watchmaker.

Audrey Hepburn will always be remembered in connection with the Tiffany's jewellery brand and her black Givenchy dress from the 1961 film *Breakfast at Tiffany's*. Hepburn became friends with Hubert de Givenchy when they met in preparation for her film *Sabrina*. Hepburn soon became his ambassador both on screen and off and the 1954 hit film was later awarded an Oscar for the film's costume designs, though Givenchy was not credited. Their friendship was to last over forty years and Hepburn wore his gowns in the 1957 film *Funny Face* and promoted the L'Interdit perfume he created for her in the same year. The French fashion designer was also closely associated with the couture of many Hollywood leading ladies and the American President John F. Kennedy's wife, Jacqueline Kennedy.

Hollywood and the film industry can wield exceptional power at brand placement. Its advocacy of branded products can elevate their reputation and appeal into iconic status. The films *The Italian Job* and *The Love Bug* both helped to strengthen the consumer affection for the mass-produced car brands, the Mini and the VW Beetle.

Stephen Fry, the English actor, writer, comedian, television presenter and all-round Apple fan attended the 2010 Apple iPad launch in London's Regent Street. He is a genuine fan of the brand and was caught up in the excitement of the launch for his favourite mobile technology company's new toy. As he wrote on his blog and now with his own 'Frypaper iPad App', he is not on Apple's payroll! He is however friends with Jonathan Ive and is kept abreast of all the latest developments and product releases from Apple. He is a self-confessed technophile and receives complimentary samples from other brands which he enthusiastically acknowledges on his website. He compares the magic of Willy Wonka and his chocolate factory with Steve Jobs and Apple.

The greatest compliment and the most credible of endorsements are made by the general public who pay for their favourite brands with their own money. The most obvious form of customer as brand ambassador is the phenomenon of the fan club. These are most evident in the fields of music, film, sport and transport. Every make and model of car or motorcycle has its own club of enthusiasts eulogizing and celebrating their favourite marque. Pop and rock bands sell t-shirts and branded merchandise so their fans can parade their logos in public. The film genre has spawned legions of Trekkies, devoted fans of *Star Trek*, and Jedi, devout fans of *Star Wars*. The highest accolade for a brand is to have its own appreciation society.

Employees as brand ambassadors

The employees of any brand are the strongest advocates of its strategy and their behaviour will reveal the truth of the brand's proposition. Each employee is an ambassador representing the brand to their colleagues, customers, suppliers and shareholders. Their interactions with the various brand audiences contribute to the overall brand experience. Therefore it makes good business sense to ensure that each member of staff is aware of the brand strategy, its history, what it stands for and their role in delivering the brand proposition.

The British Army is a fine example of a body of people working together for a common goal, aware of their individual contribution and the historical context of their regiment. Each regiment has its own history that can stretch back hundreds of years. Each British soldier is aware of their regiment's honour, their responsibility to their fellow soldiers and the purpose of their deployment. When the media question soldiers about their role, they typically receive a clear, direct and consistent response. Each regiment has a story to tell, how it was formed, the campaigns it has served in, the triumphs and losses. The insignia, the ranks, the uniform and equipment are all elements of their strong identity but the most distinctive characteristic that identifies the personnel is their unwavering spirit of camaraderie.

The quality of customer service is a differentiator for high street retail brands. When you approach the checkout counter at any Waitrose branch of the supermarket chain, you are immediately acknowledged and asked if you would like help with your packing. This courteous and friendly behaviour is a service differentiator. The staff are all partners in the retail brand and take a share in the profits. Their behaviour sets them apart from other retailers and the brand is celebrated for its helpful employees.

Waterstone's, the bookseller, was founded in 1982 by Tim Waterstone. The first branch in the UK opened in London's Old Brompton Road. What set the store apart was their employees' high standard of customer service, knowledge and enthusiasm. The booksellers in each branch make personal recommendations handwritten on tickets which are displayed on the shelves next to their favourite books. This personal touch communicates a genuine passion for books that adds integrity to their brand.

In 2010, the independent watchdog and magazine *Which?* declared the Lakeland retail group as Britain's best shop, an honour it shares with consumer electronics brand Richer Sounds. Both Lakeland and Richer Sounds are renowned for the helpful attitude and enthusiasm of their staff. Lakeland began in 1963 by selling sacks for animal feed and grew as a family business to its current position as the home of creative kitchenware. The employees are referred to as colleagues and are encouraged to treat the customers as they would want to be treated themselves. Lakeland have a Customer Ambassador who tests the products and evaluates new additions to the product line.

Branded organizations are increasingly running internal training exercises and marketing campaigns to raise their employees' awareness of their brand's ethos and history. Upholding the brand's values requires an understanding from all parties within the organization. Brands are brought to life by the experiences they provide and people are a critical factor in that experience. Consequently careless behaviour by employees can have a long-lasting impact on customer relationships with the brand.

Employees have to have someone to look up to, and the natural role model is the brand's champion, its Managing Director or Chief Executive Officer. Employees are more likely to embrace the brand if they are set a good example by their leadership. Employees can only advocate the brand when it is fully understood. Newsletters, intranets, emails and meetings should disseminate the brand message to all staff. Employees are the face of a corporate brand and happy, confident individuals who feel valued and motivated become the best recruitment campaign for the brand.

External brand ambassadors

When brands outsource and work with suppliers in partnerships they need to consider their partners' standards. If the supplier's ethics are incompatible with the brand it could have ramifications on the integrity of their brand strategy. If a supplier is profiting from inhumane working practices and poor employee or even animal welfare it will affect the brand's reputation. These people are also advocates of the brand and their welfare can have a significant impact on the brand's perception.

The practice of outsourcing telephone call centres to international locations is a delicate subject. Some call centres have gone to great efforts to train their staff and educate them in the culture of the customers they help. However, if the customer experience is less than satisfactory the brand will fall short of its expectation.

Some brands are proving to be very creative in their strategy to reach a specific audience. The energy drink brand Red Bull created a network of Student Brand Managers (SBM) to advocate the brand to fellow students. The SBM's role is concerned with bringing the brand to life through events aimed at the student community. Red Bull SBMs must be enthusiastic, creative and have lots of energy. The brand appoints people who, love life, are natural leaders and know how to balance work with play. The role gives students valuable experience of working with a top brand and the advocates get a well stocked fridge for their dormitory.

Another significant area of brand advocacy is the outsourced brand ambassador for special events. Exhibitions, brand launches and events are often run by independent professional event management companies. They will work with the brand to deliver an experience that brings the brand to life. It could include becoming part of the team on an exhibition stand, providing hospitality on behalf of the brand or even creating a themed brand experience.

Brand ambassadors can bring the brand to life and help connect the audience to its ethos. They have an important responsibility to uphold the brand's reputation and provide a personal connection to its customers.

TEST YOURSELF

▶ What is a brand ambassador?

▶ Can you name three celebrity brand ambassadors and what qualities they bring to the brand?

▶ What is 'the halo effect'?

▶ Which brand fan club are you a member of?

▶ Can you describe the brand strategy of your current employer?

▶ Can you think of a high-profile brand where its employees have failed to deliver the brand experience?

▶ Can you name three high street retailers whose employees are fine ambassadors of their brand?

13

Brand standards

In this chapter you will learn about:
- *the brand book*
- *brand guidelines*

Communicating the brand

Building a new brand is a considerable undertaking that requires the full backing of an organization's senior management and the advocacy of its employees. A brand is one of the most valuable assets an organization can have, symbolizing its reputation, experience and expectation. To succeed, the brand strategy will require the complete belief of its employees and it will be powerless if it only stays in the minds of the management team. It needs to be shared and made accessible to the whole organization.

The brand book and the brand guidelines are essential tools for disseminating the brand idea. The brand book is an uplifting manifesto designed to illuminate the brand and create awareness. The brand guideline manual is a toolkit for implementing the brand.

The brand book and brand guidelines are usually designed and produced by the creative brand consultancy that was responsible for the creative brand strategy. It is a natural progression of their brief to conclude the brand project with an instruction manual for the new brand. This is often the cut-off point for their involvement, and the day-to-day implementation of the brand may be passed to specialist agencies for marketing, advertising, packaging, retail interiors and exhibitions. These specialist creative agencies will expect to be given a copy of the brand book and brand guidelines and will be experienced at developing campaigns that reflect their client's brands.

Brand awareness

The brand book and brand guidelines should be supported with an internal awareness campaign and brought to life through workshops and training exercises. Everyone on the payroll of an organization should have a good level of understanding about the brand they are working for and its relevance to their situation. A consistent brand identity is a statement of intention and poor application of the brand communicates an unprofessional message. If a brand is to be respected then you must take care of the brand.

In Chapter 9 we described two creative exercises to encourage lateral thinking about the brand. The 'on brand – off brand' exercise is useful for engaging employees in a discussion about what constitutes 'on brand' behaviour in relation to their daily work. It can help employees to think about their specific role and how it impacts the brand. We also recommend the 'mood board' exercise from Chapter 9. This can help facilitate a discussion encouraging the employees to contribute ideas about their understanding of the brand.

The brand book

When a business invests in building a brand it is in their interest to protect their asset. As new employees join an organization they should be inducted into the brand's philosophy and educated in its meaning and values. A brand book is an essential tool for connecting employees with the brand.

The brand book is the brand manifesto. It does not necessarily have to be a physical book but the important point is that a channel of communication is made available for sharing the brand strategy. It could be a website, intranet, extranet, a PDF, a magazine, a newsletter or whichever medium is most appropriate and effective at reaching the target audience. The aim is to create a motivating and engaging method of sharing the brand idea. It should be an inspirational book that characterizes the brand and excites people to its potential. The goal is to spread awareness of the brand strategy and get the team to buy-in to the brand.

If the brand book is to succeed it should be perceived as adding value to the organization and used as a source of inspiration. There are many creative and tactile examples of brand books with high production values, printed on unusual materials in various shapes and forms. When pride and care is taken in creating the brand book the message is clear that the management are proud of the brand and are investing in their employees to become their brand ambassadors.

We suggest that both the marketing department and human resources department take an active role in the authoring of the brand book. Employee morale and team spirit can be promoted by an uplifting brand book.

The brand book contents should include a message from the brand champion and a clear explanation of the brand strategy:

- **Purpose** – *what the brand does.*
- **Vision** – *the brand's ambition.*
- **Values** – *what the brand stands for.*
- **Mission statement** – *how the brand is going to achieve its vision.*
- **Proposition** – *why you need the brand.*
- **Position** – *the brand's position in relation to its competitors.*
- **Personality** – *the brand's character.*
- **Audience** – *the people who are interested in the brand.*

The brand book should explain the cultural aspects of the brand, inviting employees to endorse the brand through their behaviour and conduct. This of course sounds like political propaganda and many employees may be suspicious or cynical. Any brand programme must be tackled with sensitivity and not be heavy handed. The brand book is not for brainwashing employees – it is for encouraging *esprit de corps*. The simple truth is that if everybody pulls together the brand will be more successful and make more profit for the organization.

The Little Red Book

The biggest selling book written in the twentieth century was *Quotations from Chairman Mao Zedong*, more popularly known as *The Little Red Book*. It bears many similarities to a brand book. It explains the principles behind the movement, the importance of working together in a united vision and respect for your fellow workers. Mao's book has enjoyed total sales second only to the Bible, which is not so surprising as it was required reading for every Chinese citizen during the Cultural Revolution. It acquired iconic status and propaganda posters featured workers clutching copies of the book. Following the death of Mao its influence dropped and it became associated with the cult of Mao's personality.

The purpose of the brand book is to inspire employees through their freewill and not to groom them into passive submission. The brand must have integrity and be authentic for it to attract the willing advocacy of its employees. Reluctant adherence to a set of rules and regulations will make a workforce indifferent to the brand and turn them into poor ambassadors.

Scouting for Boys

Scouting for Boys – A Handbook for Instruction in Good Citizenship by Lord Robert Baden-Powell is in effect the Scout movement's brand book and was first published in 1908. In 2010, television survival expert Bear Grylls is the organization's brand champion. He is the ideal role model, leading by example, and was himself a Cub Scout. *Scouting for Boys* is one of the top ten global bestselling books of all time. It explains the scouting ethos – when Lord Robert Baden-Powell wrote *Scouting for Boys* he created the template for future generations of Scouts. The book includes the movement's vision and values through the Scouts' Oath and Scouts' Law, and outlines its visual identity with a description of the uniform. The book encourages team spirit with songs and games; the Scouts' brand is practised through good health, chivalry, life-saving techniques and good citizenship. The book is inspirational and promotes self-reliance, confidence and good character. The publication helped to grow the organization into a worldwide movement and its core message is still relevant to the scouting brand today. Stephen Spielberg's all action Hollywood character and icon for adventure, Indiana Jones, was a Boy Scout who attained the distinction of Life Scout. Both Spielberg and the actor Harrison Ford, who is famous for the role of Jones, were Boy Scouts in real life.

Among the bestselling books of all time, the global top ten is noticeably biased towards self-improvement, belief and respect for mankind. The brand book aims to inspire employees to do the best they can to deliver the perfect brand. A few well-chosen words can move people to achieve greatness.

Nelson Mandela

Nelson Mandela helped inspire the South African national rugby team to win the Rugby World Cup in 1995 through the power of words. He alledgedly gave the Springbok Captain François Pienaar a copy of the speech by US President Theodore Roosevelt titled 'The Man in the Arena'. During his years of incarceration on Robben Island, Mandela himself had found encouragement in the words of a Victorian poem 'Invictus' (Latin for 'unconquered'), written by Englishman William Ernest Henley in 1875. If words can inspire a rugby team to win against the odds and encourage a great man to prevail through hardship, then a well-written brand book should inspire an organization to build a great brand.

A brand can be a sporting side, a political party, a charity, a nation as well as a company, product or service. Brands provide employment and affect the livelihood and welfare of us all.

Brand guidelines

The brand guidelines are for use by everyone whose responsibility it is to produce new marketing material for the brand. The brand guidelines will explain the basic elements of the brand identity and how to use them to create consistent branded communication.

The brand strategy and brand identity will need to be explained and shared with the relevant third parties who are given responsibility for its reproduction. From stationery to signage, vehicle livery to retail environments all these items need to be created to reflect the brand. Design groups, advertising agencies, sign writers and interior designers will need guidance on what they can or cannot do in the name of the brand. Hence the necessity for helpful guidelines and a brand book to express the brands ethos.

Some brand consultants view a logo as an immutable form, sitting in its protective zone of white space, representing all that the brand stands for. There is another school of thought that sees the logo as a transparent vessel for the containment of imagery allowing the brand to reveal its many facets (for example the Sky, Waterstones and London 2012 Olympics brand identities). The ability to implement a transient brand identity successfully depends on familiarity and context. A constantly morphing logo for a small to medium-sized business could lose its impact if it only has a limited exposure to its audiences and consequently this approach to brand identity could lead to confusion.

The brand guidelines should be recognized as a valuable resource and given a high status in any organization. The guidelines should be the first point of reference when planning any new project that carries the brand's endorsement, from printed business cards to corporate buildings. The guidelines will carry the authority of top-level management and include an opening letter of endorsement from the Chief Executive Officer (CEO). The letter is a motivational message from the brand champion, placing the brand in context with the organization's success.

Depending on the size of the organization, an individual or department should be identified as the brand guardian with responsibility for the day-to-day protection of the brand and its implementation. This responsibility of stewardship usually falls under the marketing department.

The brand guidelines are designed to make life easier; they are one less thing for busy employees to worry about and there is no excuse not to use them. Their use may be enforced with the proviso that if they are not followed the guilty department may have to destroy the incorrectly branded item and re-create it in the correct style as suggested by the guidelines. This may sound draconian, but a poorly branded item may be interpreted as counterfeit or evidence of an organization with sloppy standards. It is important to enforce the guidelines or they will lack gravitas.

The brand guidelines should be written and directed by the creative brand consultants in conjunction with the marketing department.

SUGGESTED LIST OF CHAPTERS FOR A BOOK OF BRAND GUIDELINES

- *Message from brand champion.*
- *Introduction to brand guardians and their contact details.*
- *The brand strategy:*
    - *Purpose – what the brand does.*
    - *Vision – the brand's ambition.*
    - *Values – what the brand stands for.*
    - *Mission statement – how the brand is going to achieve its vision.*
    - *Proposition – why you need the brand.*
    - *Position – the brand's position in relation to its competitors.*

> ▷ *Personality – the brand's character.*
> ▷ *Audience – the people who are interested in the brand.*
- ▶ *The brand identity basic elements:*
  > ▷ *brand name*
  > ▷ *strapline*
  > ▷ *logo*
  > ▷ *mascot (if relevant)*
  > ▷ *colour*
  > ▷ *typography*
  > ▷ *tone of voice and look and feel*
  > ▷ *divisions, departments and sub-brands (if relevant).*
- ▶ *Stationery and templates.*
- ▶ *Literature styles – brochures, leaflets, directories and reports.*
- ▶ *Typographic grids and templates.*
- ▶ *Packaging.*
- ▶ *Digital media – website, intranet, extranet, blog.*
- ▶ *Presentations – proposals and PowerPoint.*
- ▶ *Advertising.*
- ▶ *Exhibitions – trade shows, pop-up stands, banners.*
- ▶ *Signage – internal and external constructed and textile flags.*
- ▶ *Vehicle livery.*
- ▶ *Uniforms.*
- ▶ *Merchandise – t-shirts, caps, badges, pens etc.*

The above list for a book of brand guidelines is by no means complete. The scope and depth of guidance will depend entirely on the size of the brand operation.

Each chapter will require detailed examples, explanations and templates where needed. Some aspects to consider are as follows:

Print: Print specifications will include details about the paper stock, paper colour, size and weight for each item.

Visuals: Notional visuals will be required for all items including brochures, packaging, presentations, websites and advertising. The job of the guidelines is to give guidance to specialists regarding the brand's style but not to do their job for them. The aim is to direct the third party so that when they create new items for the brand they retain the brand's look, feel and tone of voice.

Signage: Vinyls and paints for architectural applications, sign writing and vehicle liveries can follow other colour matching systems to the Pantone Matching System (PMS). It is necessary to provide the relevant colour specifications as required. For example, powder-coated paint finishes and varnishes are matched to the German RAL system (*Reichsausschuß für Lieferbedingungen und Gütesicherung*) and coloured vinyls can have their own colour swatches unique to the manufacturer.

Interior design materials: Retail interiors and offices will require guidance on floor coverings (wood, tiles or carpet, etc.), wall finishes (painted, papered or clad, etc.), shelving, displays, point of sale, furniture etc. A notional guide will be required to set the look, feel and tone of voice for a typical retail outlet or office. Specialist interior designers can then interpret these guidelines. It is impossible to create a multipurpose template applicable to every situation. The brand consultant will provide guidance on the look and feel of a typical retail or office environment with a palette of materials.

Promotional merchandise: It's advisable to give guidance on the quality of merchandise. This category can include promotional giveaways designed to promote the brand. This is a vulnerable area where the brand's integrity can be compromised by a cheap object. A simple giveaway like a pen can say so much about the brand. Promotional catalogues are full of hundreds of different styles of pens that can be customized with your logo. The wrong pen can immediately cheapen your brand. The guidelines should advise on the quality and style of typical merchandise items including apparel, umbrellas and desk accessories.

ARTWORK REPRODUCTION AND DIGITAL FILES

The brand book and the brand guidelines are essential tools for disseminating the brand, but they will not be much help without artwork. Generally the creative brand consultancy will be working on an Apple operating system and so will the majority of specialist creative agencies from packaging, interiors, advertising and exhibitions. The most common business operating system is Microsoft Windows and the provision of artwork will have to take into account both platforms.

Both platforms have significant differences and it is important to compare the monitors of a PC and a Mac to see the difference in colour reproduction; websites can also reveal differences. The designer's responsibility is to check all artwork files and digital templates on their respective platforms before distributing them for use. Software programs are constantly being updated and so the provision of common file formats must take into account the availability and widespread use of application software.

A decision must be made on who will be the gatekeeper monitoring access of the digital artwork files or whether to make them universally available. The important point is that guidelines for their correct application are made available together with the artwork. What must be made clear is that these files must never be customized, altered or interfered with in any way. They have been created and made available for use for the single purpose of maintaining the brand's visual integrity. Any manipulation of the logo, including combining it with foreign elements, will contravene the brand's authority.

The Adobe suite of software applications are the industry standard software for brand identity artwork. The brand logo master artwork will most likely be created in the vector drawing application Adobe Illustrator. From the master artwork a variety of formats and colour options will be generated for specific uses.

The logo artwork will typically be made available for reproduction in the following colour options:

▶ *Pantone Matching System (PMS) spot colour.*
▶ *Four-colour process – cyan, magenta, yellow and black (CMYK).*
▶ *Black and white.*

▶ *Reversed out (white for contrast against dark backgrounds) – this is optional.*

There are myriad file options available for saving artwork, and you need to think about which ones you should use – JPEG, GIF, TIFF, PNG, BMP and WMF are some of the most common file types in use.

VECTOR GRAPHIC IMAGES

Vector Graphics are the preferred medium for creating brand logo artwork. Vector Graphic images are scalable line art graphics based on mathematically plotted curves and lines and can be enlarged or reduced without loss of quality. Adobe Illustrator is the most popular vector drawing application and is an ideal tool for creating master versions of brand artwork. To use vector graphics in third-party software applications it is necessary to save the image in the relevant file format.

EPS

Encapsulated Postscript files (EPS) are the preferred file format for brand logo artwork and can be imported into most professional publishing software applications. Vector images are usually saved in this format as they retain the scalability of the vector image without loss of sharpness. The printing of EPS images will require Adobe PostScript software. Bitmap or raster images may also be saved in this format.

BITMAP OR RASTER GRAPHIC IMAGES

Bitmap or raster graphic images are ideally suited to photographs and continuous tone images that feature gradual shifts in tone and colour. These images are resolution dependent and may not be enlarged without loss of quality.

GIF

The Graphics Interchange Format (GIF) is meant only for use in displaying graphics on websites and is not suitable for photographic images. This bitmapped image file format was developed by the internet service provider Compuserve to facilitate the cross-platform viewing of images online. It was designed for the web and has a limited RGB (red, green, blue) colour palette of 256 colours, making it unsuitable for photographs. It is typically used for text-based images including menu titles, buttons and animation sequences for online use.

PNG

The Portable Network Graphics (PNG) file is meant only for use in displaying graphics on websites. It is a bitmapped image format that was designed to improve on the GIF format. It has a larger RGB colour palette but does not support animation.

JPEG

The Joint Photographic Experts Group (JPEG) file is ideal for onscreen use and is widely used in web design. The majority of digital cameras automatically save photographs in this file format and it is great for delivering high image quality at low file sizes. However, this file format is not suitable for text-based images or line drawings. It supports both CMYK (cyan, magenta, yellow, black) and RGB (red, green, blue) formats.

TIFF

The Tag Image File Format (TIFF) is ideal for printing photographic images and provides the highest possible quality for continuous tone photographic images. It produces large file sizes but is commonly exchangeable across different computer platforms.

WMF

The Windows Metafile Format (WMF) is ideal for use in Microsoft applications like Word and PowerPoint. It can include both vector and bitmap content and was developed by Microsoft for use in its suite of software products.

Insight

It is essential that the brand guardian is aware of the different digital file formats and how to apply them. It is their responsibility to ensure that the correct artwork is provided for the required job. From experience, the JPEG file format is the most commonly requested logo digital artwork file

format despite its resolution dependence and unsuitability
for reproducing solid colour or sharp-edged typography. The
challenge to the brand guardian is to educate their suppliers
and colleagues to use the right files. If the supplier is unable to
use a vector art file, such as an EPS, it may be a sign that they
are not using professional graphics software applications.

COLOUR

The brand identity colour palette will be identified by a Pantone
Matching System (PMS) colour reference. Pantone is the *de facto*
colour matching system for graphic designers and printers. The
system has standardized ink colours to facilitate consistent colour
matches. Pantone sell a range of swatch books identifying the
PMS number and how to achieve the equivalent match from the
four-colour printing process (CMYK). With the prevalence of
the internet, the guides now include references for the equivalent
onscreen display in RGB and the closest corresponding colour for
a website in hypertext mark-up language. The challenge for the
brand guardian is to manage the closest possible colour match
across different media. The Pantone system is helpful but it is
only the beginning.

Considerations for print colour continuity

A solid Pantone colour ink or 'special colour' can produce different
results depending on the density of the ink solid printed onto the
paper, the weight and quality of the paper stock and the surface
finish, for example laminated or varnished. If you print the same
design on a range of different white papers or card stocks you will
get subtle tonal differences in the ink colour match.

The differences between solid Pantone colour inks and their four-
colour process (CMYK) equivalents are very noticeable. A poor
match between the Pantone solid ink and its CMYK equivalent
can provide disappointing results. When printing in four colour
it may prove necessary to print the corporate brand colour as a
special Pantone (PMS) spot colour ink. This is always advisable
when printing large areas of solid colour in the brand palette.

This increases the cost of printing a design by adding an extra print plate to the four-colour process but it will always provide superior results. An alternative is to choose a corporate brand colour that is acceptable in CMYK and this can pay dividends in reduced printing costs. The careful brand guardian will keep samples of each printed job so that they can use them as a record of colour continuity on different paper stocks and surface finishes.

Considerations for onscreen colour continuity

The differences between designs displayed on an Apple Mac computer and a PC running Microsoft Windows can be quite noticeable. It is essential that designers specifying corporate colour references for onscreen display compare the two platforms before finalizing the colour specification. In the infancy of the internet, web graphics were limited to a palette of 216 safe colours that could be guaranteed to display across platforms. This was due to the prevalence of 8-bit video cards, which limited the display of colour, but this restriction is now obsolete due to advances in technology. It's always a good idea to check and compare results on different platforms and models to get a true picture of how the general public will view the final website or onscreen presentation.

TYPOGRAPHY

A corporate typeface will increase brand recognition and give greater control over the brand's identity. The choices include a licensed font or a specifically designed typeface for the brand. If the budget does not stretch to a global licence then it will be necessary to make a selection from the universally available typefaces common to Microsoft Windows users. This list is often referred to as browser safe fonts and is adopted by web designers so that they can safely specify websites to display the same typefaces. Browser safe typefaces include Arial, Georgia, Times New Roman, Trebuchet and Verdana.

If the guidelines specify an unusual set of fonts, the supplier will need to buy a copy of the relevant corporate typefaces. The guidelines will need to include details of the appropriate Type Foundry or supplier.

TEST YOURSELF

▶ *What is the purpose of the brand book and brand guidelines?*

▶ *What would you include in a brand book?*

▶ *How would you train employees to understand their brand?*

▶ *Can you think of a motivational book that has inspired a group of people?*

▶ *What would you include in your brand guidelines?*

▶ *Name three digital graphic file formats and their uses?*

▶ *What is the difference between PMS and CMYK?*

▶ *Name three browser safe fonts?*

14

....

Brand protection

In this chapter you will learn:
- *how to protect your brand assets*
- *how to create new revenue streams from a successful brand*

Protecting your brand assets

One of the most important reasons to create a brand is to differentiate a product, service or organization from its competitors. A recognizable brand gives a customer the confidence that they are dealing with a legitimate and authentic organization. A successful brand will inevitably attract the attention of competitors who may be tempted to hi-jack the brand's success by emulating its products, services or brand personality. Counterfeiting is the illegal practice of deliberately using another person's trade mark without their consent to sell similar goods or services. It is obviously in the interest of the brand owners to legally protect their brand assets and limit the chances of competitors profiting from their brand investment. Examples of brand hi-jacking can range from using a similar name, a logo with a close likeness, the same colours or combinations, type styles, packaging shapes, product designs, technology, sounds, look, feel or even smell. In fact anything that is critical to the brand experience should be legally protected to stop competitors capitalizing on your brand.

Owning the intellectual property (IP) rights for the brand will be a significant factor in the purchase price if the owner wishes to sell the business at a later stage. The brand could be sold, licensed or franchised once the intellectual property rights have been obtained. The enforcement of trade marks and patents will help to protect the brand's status and increase its value.

Jane Winkworth, the founder of French Sole (a shoe company specializing in ballet shoes of every colour), believes that if you have a good idea and a good name, you should make sure you have a good trade mark lawyer also. It is a worthwhile long-term investment spending money on protecting your design and name.

SECURING THE BRAND NAME

One of the first and most important considerations when creating a brand identity is to decide on a name. You will need a name to set up a Limited Company – you can have a legal name separate to the trading or brand name, but generally the Limited Company name and brand name for an organization are related. In the United Kingdom a Limited Company has limited liability and is an attractive option for private businesses because personal assets are kept legally separate from the finances of the company, unlike a sole trader.

It is prudent to confirm the availability of a unique brand name before becoming too emotionally and financially committed to your choice. We advise that you check the availability of a corresponding internet domain name, ensuring that the appropriate suffix is available, for example, .com and .co.uk. If someone is already using your choice of name online it may prove difficult to use the name for your brand. Variations of the name may be possible, but they may prove harder for customers to remember or find online.

The following resources will help you check the availability of your brand name choice:

Domain name check
We recommend using the 'Domain Name Self Service' from Europe's largest corporate domain name management specialist NetNames. Using their website at www.netnames.com you can check availability for any global or country specific domain name. You can register your choice with NetNames or with your internet service provider (ISP).

Social media check
Online social media, including Twitter, Facebook and YouTube, play an important part in brand awareness. We would recommend checking these and other sites for the availability of your brand name. The 'KnowEm' online resource at www.knowem.com allows you to check if your brand name is available on all the most popular social media websites.

Limited Company check
The Companies House website at www.companieshouse.co.uk provides a facility called 'WebCheck' to search for the availability of your proposed company name. The service is for UK-based companies only, but if you want to investigate companies in other countries a list of Worldwide Registries is available.

If both the domain name and Limited Company name choice are available for registration then we recommend buying the domain name to secure it and registering your Limited Company name.

INTELLECTUAL PROPERTY

The Intellectual Property Office of the United Kingdom has the following definition on their website www.ipo.gov.uk: 'Intellectual property (IP) results from the expression of an idea. So IP might be a brand, an invention, a design, a song or another intellectual creation.'

IP allows the originator to own their creations, for example a mobile phone can be completely protected using the four types of IP:

- **Trade marks:** *protect the brand name and logo of the mobile phone's manufacturer.*
- **Copyright:** *could protect the instruction booklet, publicity images and the ring tones.*
- **Registered designs:** *protect the shape and configuration of the mobile phone.*
- **Patents:** *protect the internal components and the process by which they were made.*

Trade marks

Trade marks protect the brand identity of your company, product or services and are applicable to brand names, straplines, logos and all symbols. To qualify for a trade mark the symbol or name must be distinctive and not be a generic description of the product or service. Successful registration with the UK's Intellectual Property Office qualifies the owner to display the ® symbol beside the trade mark to indicate that it cannot be used by anyone else.

- **UK:** *A UK trade mark may be applied for through the UK Intellectual Property Office at www.ipo.gov.uk.*
- **European Community:** *To apply for a trade mark which will be valid throughout the European Community, visit the Office for Harmonization in the Internal Market (OHIM) website at http://oami.europa.eu.*
- **Worldwide:** *To trade mark internationally, please visit the World Intellectual Property Organization (WIPO) website at www.wipo.int.*

Copyright

Copyright protects an original work from being copied by other people. It can be applied to original works including: art, music, literature, drama, films, broadcasts and sound recordings. Copyright does not have an official registration system in the UK or most other parts of the world. Copyright is automatic and this convention is respected internationally. It is advisable to use the © symbol together with the originator's name and date, which can help protect the original work. If you wish to use copyright protected material it will require the permission of the copyright owner or the arrangement of a licence.

Design rights

Design rights concern the shape and the visual look of an object. It is not necessary to apply for design rights as all original designs are automatically protected for 15 years from the time when the design was first recorded in a design document. A registered design will increase the protection to 25 years and will make it easier to prosecute people who copy the design.

- ▶ **UK:** *UK design rights may be applied for through the UK Intellectual Property Office at www.ipo.gov.uk.*
- ▶ **European Community:** *To protect your design throughout the European Community, visit the Office for Harmonization in the Internal Market (OHIM) website at http://oami.europa.eu.*
- ▶ **Worldwide:** *For most of the world's major nations you can make a separate application to that country for design protection.*

Patents

The processes and features that make things work are protectable by patents. Inventors profit from their inventions by patenting their ideas.

A patent means that no one will be allowed to make, use, copy, import or sell the invention without the permission of the patent holder.

- ▶ **UK:** *UK patents may be applied for through the UK Intellectual Property Office at www.ipo.gov.uk.*
- ▶ **Europe:** *To protect patents in more than 30 European countries, visit the European Patent Office (EPO) website at www.epo.org.*

- ▶ **Worldwide:** *To patent your invention internationally, visit the World Intellectual Property Organization (WIPO) website at* <u>www.wipo.int</u>.

Other types of protection

There are a variety of specific levels of brand protection that may be considered, including: confidentiality agreements, database rights, protection abroad and trade secrets. We recommend that you refer to the Intellectual Property Office for further information at <u>www.ipo.gov.uk</u>.

Insight

We strongly advise that you appoint an intellectual property (IP) lawyer to help you get the most from your intellectual property assets. Intellectual property is complicated and expert help is required. It is critical that you are properly protected in order to leverage the most from your brand.

New revenue streams

LICENSING

It takes years to build a strong brand and earn the trust and loyalty of its customers. When a customer gets into the habit of shopping for a particular brand they are more likely to try new products and services from the same company. When a brand enjoys a high level of credibility it can capitalize on its reputation by branching out into ancillary products that complement its original offering. Some of these ancillary products may not be manufactured by the parent brand but produced under licence by a third party. This strategy can be financially profitable for the brand owner and can increase the brand's equity by gaining a wider market penetration. Brand owners will naturally be protective of their hard-earned success and be aware that any compromise in quality could jeopardize their brand's status. A carefully chosen licensee must handle the brand with respect to safeguard the brand's reputation. Types of licences include: copyright, merchandising, patent and trade mark.

The entertainment industry is highly skilled at using licensing power to leverage the full potential of their intellectual property. The BBC (e.g. *Dr Who*, *Top Gear*, *In The Night Garden*), Chorion (e.g. *Mr Men*, *Noddy*, *The World of Beatrix Potter*), HIT Entertainment (e.g. *Bob the Builder*, *Thomas & Friends*, *Angelina Ballerina*) and even museums including London's V&A (Victoria & Albert) Museum are all successfully licensing their Intellectual Property assets.

Merchandise licensing

Merchandise licensing has become an important aspect of the film industry. From the latest Disney/Pixar blockbusters to the *Chronicles of Narnia*, children can't get enough of their favourite characters. Even adults are not immune to the persuasive effects of subtle product positioning. From *Iron Man* to *The Matrix*, a carefully chosen soundtrack, a tie-in book or featured product can all benefit from association with a film's success.

Star Wars

The film director George Lucas is the mastermind behind the 1977 film *Star Wars*, one of cinema's greatest successes. The film's producers, 20th Century Fox, had little idea how spectacularly popular the film would prove to be and signed away the film's merchandising rights to Lucas. This arrangement has significantly contributed to Lucas's fortune and in 2010 *Forbes* magazine attributed $17.5 billion to total merchandise receipts since 1977. This income is supported through the licensing of toy figures, books, games and associated film ephemera. He also owns LucasArts (video games) and Lucas Licensing (*Star Wars* toys and books).

Since *Star Wars*, the owners of Intellectual Property have been more aware of the licensing opportunities available to them. George Lucas demonstrated how it was possible to make a huge profit from film licensing. As with any brand it pays for the brand owner to take care of how their brand is used on merchandise. The author of the Harry Potter series, J.K. Rowling, is renowned for keeping a watchful eye on how her characters are portrayed. This strategy maintains the brand's integrity.

CAUTION: We would add a word of caution on licensing as it needs to be carried out with care and sensitivity towards the brand's values. A poor licensing agreement may stretch the brand's credibility and weaken its integrity. Over exposure can have the adverse effect of cheapening a brand and evaporating the equity that was hard won and built over time. If the brand appears on everything from water bottles to t-shirts it could burn out quickly.

FRANCHISING

When a company develops a successful branded business model they may choose to grow the brand by franchising the format. Franchising is when the owner (the franchisor) sells the rights of their branded business model to an entrepreneur (the franchisee). The franchisee usually buys the rights to use the branded business model for a specific period of time and in an agreed location. Clearly the franchisor needs to take care in selecting a suitable franchisee who will become an ambassador for the brand. The following brands are examples of successful franchises: McDonald's, Kall-Kwik and Dyno-Rod.

TEST YOURSELF

▶ *Why should you protect your brand assets?*

▶ *How can you protect your brand name?*

▶ *What is intellectual property (IP)?*

▶ *Why should a brand be trade marked?*

▶ *What is copyright?*

▶ *What is eligible for design rights protection?*

▶ *What is a patent?*

▶ *What is licensing?*

▶ *Name three types of licences?*

▶ *What is franchising?*

15

Brand delivery

In this chapter you will learn:
- *about the brand launch*
- *how to introduce your brand to the market and internal audience*

Brand launch

The brand's debut is its formal introduction into the world and the first moment that the strategy and identity are revealed in public. It's a very important occasion when the brand is delivered for the first time and lasting opinions will be formed. The occasion should be marked with all the passion and pride that went into creating the brand. Ships are launched with a naming ceremony and a bottle of champagne is broken across the bow. When the final beam of a new building is put in place the architects and contractors traditionally hold a topping out ceremony. In the United States the final beam of a skyscraper is painted white and signed with pride by the team involved. These occasions are gestures of goodwill for the future success of the enterprise, confirming the identity and aspirations of the contributing parties. If you fail to launch a brand properly, then you miss a great opportunity to galvanize the wider community. A good launch gives a brand a helping hand, guiding it in the right direction towards wider awareness and success. Like the birth of a new baby, the launch of a new brand should be a happy occasion supported by messages of goodwill. Before the good news is made public the closest relatives should be informed first and, in the case of a brand launch, that means the employees and strategic partners.

You can't be new twice, and it is advantageous to seize the moment and capitalize on the element of surprise. If a new brand rolls out slowly then it will lose its impetus and interest will wane. We have all read news reports where an insider has leaked images of a new brand before it has been properly finished and formally introduced. This can prove detrimental to the brand and may attract negative and ill-informed criticism. When new models of cars are road tested during the development stage they are usually camouflaged. Their shape is distorted with cladding to prevent the prying lenses of photographers from getting a pre-launch glimpse of the latest addition to the marque. It is equally important to keep your brand development under wraps before launching the new idea publicly.

BROADCASTING THE NEWS

The launch of a new brand is one of the greatest opportunities to attract media attention and introduce your new product, service or organization to the widest possible audience. Journalists want stories, something new and different to write about, and a brand launch will be newsworthy. A well-prepared press release submitted to the right journalists will help to create brand awareness.

The brand launch is an opportunity for management to announce the new brand, reveal its new identity and explain the strategy behind it. The internal launch of the brand must take precedence over any other announcements. The management and creative team behind the new brand should work together to agree the best method for delivering the brand to its internal audience. Ideally the brand launch will be an expression of the brand and the event will bring to life the new brand's ethos in a spirited display that captures the imagination of the employees, compelling them to take part in its future success. A large organization may appoint an events management company to organize the launch. Other specialists that can play an important ongoing role include public relations (PR), advertising and marketing. Whatever the size of the organization, it is important to ensure that the launch is an uplifting occasion that complements the brand's vision and values. As the saying goes, 'you only get one chance to make a first impression'.

Throughout this book we have looked at the aspects that define brands and how these qualities help to build market-leading products and services. The brand launch will be a proving ground in which the expectation is raised, the experience felt and the reputation built.

The event

The launch event is a poignant moment symbolic of all the passion, determination and cooperation that are necessary to realize a brand. The witnesses to this new brand will have no idea of all the hours of hard work that have gone into getting to this point. They will not know the names of the people who made their contribution at each stage from strategy to design and production. Consequently, the launch has a duty of care to their endeavours to successfully deliver the brand to the expectant audience.

Apple iPad global launch

When Steve Jobs launched Apple's new tablet computer in late January 2010 he strengthened the Apple brand and introduced a new product category in the shape of the iPad. The launch was shared internationally by a video on the Apple website.

Brand focus delivery: Creativity is at Apple's core and the brand continues to deliver genre-defining products from the iPod to the iMac and iPhone. The new iPad is no exception and the launch proved

(Contd)

that apart from being just an electronic book reader the new product offers email, web, photo album and music possibilities together with a seemingly infinite variety of Apps. Apple's support of Software Development Kits (SDKs) allows independent developers to express their creativity through Apps development.

Brand culture delivery: Steve Jobs, Apple's brand champion, introduced the iPad in his trade mark black polo-neck jersey and jeans. He reminded the audience of Apple's iconic products and the company's history. Jobs introduced the people who are the brand's ambassadors and invited them to demonstrate the product's functions. Jobs then presented the iPad's tactile qualities and the motion sensing capabilities.

Brand strategy delivery: Steve Jobs announced that Apple had evolved into a Mobile Devices brand 34 years after it launched as Apple Computers. The brand was described as being at the intersection of art and technology and Jonathan Ive spoke of how this product defined Apple's vision and their sense of what is next.

Brand identity delivery: The brand name, Apple logo and the look and feel associated with the brand were all part of the stage craft. The language was confident and positive and the presenters were informally dressed in the black top and jeans style for which Jobs is famously known.

Brand champion and brand ambassadors: Steve Jobs is very much the Apple brand champion and it is hard to imagine an Apple brand launch without his personality. The brand ambassadors were his Apple colleagues and Apps partners.

APPLE IPAD UK LAUNCH – THE CUSTOMER EXPERIENCE

Four months after the initial launch, the Apple iPad had its UK retail debut on 28 May 2010. The following experience is a first-hand account of the iPad launch at Apple's flagship store in London's Regent Street.

Expectation: The media reported that some of the most dedicated fans had queued the night before to secure their place as the first UK customers. By 10 am on Friday morning the queue had grown around the block. The customers were predominantly men in their 20s to 40s eager to become early adopters of the iPad. Some of the fans were interviewed by the attendant news organizations, including the BBC, and the atmosphere was good-natured.

Apple's brand ambassadors looked after the queue by handing out complimentary bottles of water and enthusiastically answering any questions. The Apple staff wore sky-blue t-shirts bearing the product name clearly in white with an identity lanyard around their neck.

The Apple store at 235 Regent Street is a splendid building in a prestigious location that consolidates the brand's status. Enticing images of the iPad were suspended behind the shop windows, creating desire for the product. The overall look and feel was of simplicity and elegance.

Experience: As customers came to the front of the queue, an Apple representative enthusiastically greeted them with a handshake. Customers were then clapped and applauded like celebrities as they made their way up the stairs and passed the welcoming cordon. The event was well organized and customers were looked after attentively. The event complemented the Apple brand and was a successful debut for their new product. The launch was full of energy, enthusiasm and dynamism.

Reputation: The loyalty of devoted fans was evident at the Apple iPad launch with some people willing to spend the night outside the shop in order to be the first owners. The brand's website announced that after only 80 days since its US debut the iPad had enjoyed sales of 3 million. The website stated that this new product was 'defining the future of mobile media and computing devices'.

In summary, the expectation was fulfilled, the experience was exciting and Apple's reputation was enhanced.

A consistent delivery

After the exhilaration of the brand launch it is important not to rest on your laurels and expect the brand to take care of itself. With inspired leadership, committed employees and a great product or service, the brand will grow into a valuable asset.

A consistent delivery does not mean maintaining the *status quo*; it concerns the continued relevance of the brand and its ability to adapt in an ever-changing world. The brand is the heart of the organization, product or service and everyone who is connected with the brand has their part to play in its success. The creation of a brand is an opportunity to build something new and distinct that has purpose and ambition.

We hope you will be inspired to create your perfect brand!

In the words of Mark Twain:

So throw off the bowlines.
Sail away from the safe harbor.
Catch the trade winds in your sails.
Explore. Dream. Discover.

Index